HUNTER
DAVIES'
LISTS

Researcher: Caitlin Davies

CASSELL
ILLUSTRATED

First published in Great Britain in 2004 by Cassell Illustrated,
a division of Octopus Publishing Group Limited
2-4 Heron Quays, London E14 4JP

Text copyright © 2004 Hunter Davies
Design and layout copyright © Octopus Publishing Group Ltd

A CIP catalogue record for this book is available from the British Library.

ISBN 1 84403 2450
EAN 9781844032457

Printed in Spain

HUNTER DAVIES is the author of over 30 books, several of which have become modern classics. They include the authorised biography of The Beatles, *The Glory Game*, *A Walk Around the Lakes* and *Boots, Balls and Haircuts*. As a journalist, he writes a column about money for *The Sunday Times* and a column about football for *The New Statesman*. He is married to the novelist and biographer, Margaret Forster. They have three children.

CAITLIN DAVIES is the author of a novel called *Jamestown Blues* and a non-fiction book called *The Return of El Negro*. She is now writing a memoir of her life in Southern Africa, to be published in 2005. She is also a freelance journalist, regularly writing education features for the *Independent*. She has a daughter called Ruby and a dog called Slobber.

CONTENTS

~

Introduction

As we stagger through life, we all make lists. It's one of the signs of human behaviour – as soon as they had crawled out of their caves, humans were compiling lists of animals hunted and their favourite words.

Lists, roughly speaking, come in three types. Some are mental props written either on scraps of paper or in our heads, listing jobs to be done, objects to be acquired, actions to be taken. These are functional lists, serving a specific purpose. Then there are factual lists, detailing globules of information that don't necessarily require any action to be taken: facts roughly connected and set out in an order, or just all the facts gathered on the same subject, in no particular order. Then there are lists that are just opinions: my favourite puddings, my best Beatles' singles, my top films, my worst holiday, people I really really fancy.

If those are the three basic types of list, we then come to an interesting subdivision: male lists and female lists. Women, on the whole, are mainly concerned with lists as mental aids, listing vital things to be done, presents to be bought, meals to be cooked. They have so many things to remember that out of necessity rather than whimsy they create lists. The very process of writing the list seems to help clear their minds. Often, they will make a list after they have done all the jobbies – writing out the list, then ticking off things already done, feeling really pleased, even though nobody knows. Strange.

The second type of list, factual, tends to be a mainly male preserve. Sports records are the obvious example, or all their CDs, in alphabetical order. Is it because men are trying to gain control over their life – or trying to escape it? Or are they simply anoraks?

The third type of list, based on opinions, is again almost wholly male: England's best-ever strikers or their favourite childhood TV shows. I was in the kitchen of a young couple recently, and their noticeboard had two lists – one listed flour, something for nits, tights, birthday card, gas board. The other listed Owen, Rooney, Beckham, Campbell, anyone but Gary Neville. Each list was ongoing, being deleted and added to every day, destined forever to go their separate ways.

I've always loved lists, of any sort, trivial or otherwise. My oldest surviving list, made as an adult, now kept in the pages of our family

Bible, was when our first child was about to be born and I was listing possible names – Caitlin, Morag, Kirsten, Amanda, Lucy or Mark, Gavin, Simon, Callum, Saul, Adam. They reflect the popular names back in the 1960s. My wife looks at the list now and says, 'Impossible, I could never have wanted the name Morag, that must have been you.'

In 1980 I published a book called *The British Book of Lists*. It was partly a pinch from a similar American book, which contained just American lists, but also a way of clearing out and using up all the daft lists and odd facts I had accumulated over the years. I also thought of new lists and hired people short of a few pennies to ring firms such as Marks & Spencer to find out what their best-selling items were the previous week (chicken first, then ladies' jumpers). I also asked my neighbour, the late A.J.P. Taylor, to make a list of Prime Ministers who had been adulterers. Little did I know this list would ever be added to. The book was a big success and for the next few years came out in many reprints and new editions, including a children's version for charity.

Twenty-five years later, the world is awash with lists. Government and official departments are obsessed with churning out the latest figures to show how well they are doing; the Internet is loaded with lists, many of them unreliable, not to say dodgy. On TV, radio, newspapers, magazines and from corporate bodies all over the globe, endless lists are being turned out, but disguised as news, surveys, research and opinion polls.

This modest little offering is meant as light reading, a stocking-filler, an amusement while travelling. I am grateful to my daughter Caitlin, who as a little girl helped on the first edition and is now an author in her own right, for doing most of the real hard work.

The lists are different, because the world is different and our interests have changed. We have steered away from many of the factual types of lists we created last time, which are now commonplace, done by everyone, so, alas, no more Marks & Spencer chicken...

HUNTER DAVIES, LONDON NW5, JUNE 2004

**Some damning reviews
and comments**

**Classic songs
and their origins**

**Some modern
classic records
and their origins**

TV footage

**Most complained-about
advertisements**

UK's top crime writers

Great *Guardian* corrections

Most stolen artists

THE
ARTS
AND
MEDIA

Some damning reviews and comments

On authors, composers and artists who went on,
surprisingly, to be pretty well thought of nonetheless
by posterity.

AUTHORS

J.M. Barrie: 'Oh, for an hour of Herod.' Novelist Anthony Hope, after the first night of *Peter Pan*.

A.A. Milne: 'I see no future for Mr A.A. Milne, whose plots are as thin as a filleted anchovy.' Critic H. Dennis Bradley, 1925.

Samuel Beckett: 'I've been brooding in my bath and it is my considered opinion that *Waiting for Godot* is the end of theatre as we know it.' Actor Robert Morley.

Lord Byron: 'We counsel him to forthwith abandon poetry.' *Edinburgh Review*.

William Wordsworth: 'This, we think, has the merit of being the very worst poem we ever saw printed in a quarto volume.' Lord Jeffrey in the *Edinburgh Review* on Wordsworth's *The White Doe of Rylstone*, 1815.

Joseph Conrad: 'I cannot abide Conrad's souvenir-shop style, bottled ships and shell necklaces of romantic clichés.' Russian novelist Vladimir Nabokov.

D.H. Lawrence: 'Filth. Nothing but obscenities.' Joseph Conrad.

Charles Dickens: 'It would take a heart of stone not to laugh aloud at the death of Little Nell.' Oscar Wilde.

Thomas Hardy: 'When I finished the story I opened the windows and let the fresh air in.' American critic, anon., on *Jude the Oscure*.

Henry James: 'An idiot, and a Boston idiot to boot, than which there is nothing lower in the world.' Writer H.L. Mencken.

James Joyce: 'James Joyce is rather inaudible because he is talking to himself.' G.K. Chesterton.

Jack Kerouac: 'That's not writing, that's typing.' Truman Capote.

Norman Mailer: 'It's a fake. A clever, talented, admirably executed fake.' Gore Vidal on *The Naked and the Dead*.

Abraham Lincoln: 'The President acted without sense, so let us pass over his silly remarks.' *The Patriot*, Harrisburg, on Lincoln's Gettysburg Address.

COMPOSERS

Beethoven: 'Beethoven always sounds to me like the upsetting of bags of nails.' John Ruskin.

Berlioz: 'This is the way Berlioz composes – he splutters the ink over the pages of ruled paper and the result is as chance wills it.' Frédéric Chopin.

Chopin: 'The entire works of Chopin present a motley surface of ranting hyperbole and excruciating cacophony.' *Musical World*, 1841.

Haydn: 'A mere fop...a scribbler of songs.' Gregorious Werner, contemporary composer.

Gustav Mahler: 'A detailed annotation of what the music would be like if only the composer could think of the right notes.' *Musical Times*, 1931, on Mahler's Symphony No. 2.

Puccini: 'The opera has been produced with great success in...Italy and South America...and as far as I am concerned, the places are welcome to it.' *Morning Post*, 1906, on *Tosca*.

Schubert: 'Perhaps a more overrated man never existed.' *Musical Times*, 1897.

Tchaikovsky: 'His first piano concerto, like the first pancake, is a flop.' Russian critic Nicolai Soloviev.

Richard Wagner: 'Wagner has good moments, but bad quarter-hours.' Gioacchino Rossini.

ARTISTS

Degas: 'Degas is nothing but a peeping tom.' *The Churchman*, May 1886.

Jacob Epstein: 'Stone-carving doesn't happen to be what he's best at.' Fellow sculptor Eric Gill.

Henry Moore: 'The statues are hideous beyond words.' *Morning Post*, 1929.

Paul Gaugin: 'All of his figures have a smutty look.' John Burroughs.

Monet: 'It is only too easy to catch people's attention by doing something worse than anyone has dared to do it before.' Anon. reviewer in *Charivari*.

J.M.W. Turner: 'This brown thing – is this your Turner?' Monet.

Augustus John: 'The latest paintings are worthless. There is less talent than trick.' Art critic Clive Bell, *New Statesman*, June 1938.

Whistler: 'I have heard much of cockney impudence before now, but never expected to hear a coxcomb ask 200 guineas for flinging a pot of paint in the public's face.' John Ruskin.

Picasso: 'If I met Picasso in the street, I would kick him in the pants.'
Sir Alfred Munnings, President of the Royal Academy.

Graham Sutherland: 'It makes me look half-witted, which I aint.'
Winston Churchill, on his portrait by Sutherland.

Classic songs and their origins

SUMMER IS ICUMEN IN, 1240: Thought to be our oldest existing
popular song. Written by John of Fornsette, a monk at Reading, on
hearing the first cuckoo of the year.

GREENSLEEVES, c.1540: Mentioned by Shakespeare in *The Merry
Wives of Windsor*. Allegedly composed by Henry VIII.

GOLDEN SLUMBERS, c.1600: Original words by Thomas Dekker.
Paul McCartney had fun with the words on 'Abbey Road', but used his
own tune.

POP GOES THE WEASEL, 1620: Created by the Pilgrim Fathers as a
singing game, later adopted by London hatters. In 1961 Anthony
Newley turned it into a Top 20 hit.

THE FIRESHIP, c.1650: A sea shanty that became *The Rakish Kind* and
then a 1951 hit for Guy Mitchell as *The Roving Kind*.

BARBARA ALLEN, 1666, which was when Samuel Pepys mentioned it
in his diary, so it's presumably even older.

I GAVE MY LOVE A CHERRY, 1680: Also known as *The Riddle Song*.
Melody later used by Donny Osmond for *The Twelfth of Never*.

HARK THE HERALD ANGELS SING, 1739: Words written by Charles
Wesley, but since lifted onto millions of Christmas cards.

GOD SAVE THE QUEEN, or KING, as the case may be, 1745: Written as a battlecry for the House of Hanover. Words by Henry Carey. The more triumphalist verses have now been quietly dropped.

GOD REST YOU MERRY GENTLEMEN, 1770: Interesting from a punctuation point of view – was originally: 'God rest you merry, gentlemen', but the comma and the original sense got lost.

AULD LANG SYNE, 1789, which was when Robert Burns added the words, but the tune dates back to 1687. Sung throughout the civilised world on New Year's Eve – especially Millennium eve.

SILENT NIGHT, 1818: A young Austrian priest, Joseph Mohr, wrote the words after visiting a woodcutter's wife who had just given birth. The village organist added a tune.

ABIDE WITH ME, 1847: One Sunday, the Rev. Henry Francis Lyte preached a sermon, wrote this hymn – and then died.

WAY DOWN UPON THE SWANNEE RIVER, 1852: Written by Stephen Foster. He had never seen the Swannee – just liked the name.

JINGLE BELLS, 1857: Written by a Boston teacher, James Pierpont, for a Sunday school Christmas show.

D'YE KEN JOHN PEEL, 1869, which was when William Metcalfe, choirmaster at Carlisle Cathedral, wrote the tune we now know. The words were written in 1829 by John Woodcock Graves in honour of his friend John Peel, a famous Caldbeck huntsman. Now sung by huntsmen, and Cumbrians, everywhere.

SWING LOW, SWEET CHARIOT, 1872: Written by Sarah Sheppard after being talked out of suicide. Originally 'Swing Down, Sweet Chariot'. African slave workers had visions of chariots sweeping down to take them to heaven. Now England's adopted rugby song.

HAPPY BIRTHDAY TO YOU, 1893: The song was actually composed, not taken out of the air, by two American sisters and nursery teachers, Mildred and Patty Hill. Originally 'Good Morning to You'. Later changed to Happy Birthday. Used by Western Union in the 1930s as a singing telegram, until they were sued for breach of copyright.

Source: Brother, Can you spare a dime?, *Spencer Leigh, 2000*

Some modern classic records and their origins

YOU'LL NEVER WALK ALONE, 1945: Written by Rodgers and Hammerstein for their musical *Carousel.* Sinatra and Judy Garland did quite well with it at the time, but it was Gerry and the Pacemakers' version in 1963 that turned it into Liverpool's and then football's anthem.

ROCK AROUND THE CLOCK, 1955: Bill Haley and the Comets. Haley was 30 at the time, but looked older, plump and decidedly unsexy, with a silly quiff. It was the song's inclusion in the teen film *Blackboard Jungle*, causing kids in the USA and UK to dance in the aisles and tear up seats, which made it a worldwide hit. Now seen as arguably the first rock'n'roll record.

MY WAY, 1967: English words written by Paul Anka to an existing French tune. Frank Sinatra first recorded it in 1969 – and it became his anthem, although he later came to dislike it.

CANDLE IN THE WIND, 1974: Elton John with words by Bernie Taupin. Song was originally a tribute to Marilyn Monroe, addressing her by her real name, Norma Jean, but the words were altered in 1997 in memory of Diana, Princess of Wales, and performed at her funeral in Westminster Abbey by Elton John.

LOVE IS ALL AROUND, 1967: A minor period hit for that very 1960s group The Troggs. Reg Presley said he knocked it out in 15 minutes. Didn't really become a smash hit till it was used in *Four Weddings and a Funeral* in 1994.

NO WOMAN, NO CRY, 1975: Recorded live by Bob Marley and the Wailers at the Lyceum in London. Written by Marley, remembering his life in Trenchtown, Jamaica. Helped make him the first reggae singer to become a world superstar.

THRILLER, 1983: Michael Jackson. The title of his album, which became the best-selling album of all time, with 35 million copies sold. Helped along by a 14-minute dance video, which generated more interest than the song itself.

EVERY BREATH YOU TAKE, 1983: Sting. Written by him in Jamaica, while staying at Goldeneye, Ian Fleming's old house. Unable to sleep, he got up in the night and wrote it.

YESTERDAY, 1965: The Beatles. Paul McCartney says the song came to him in a dream. When he woke up, he wrote it down as 'Scrambled eggs, oh my baby how I love your legs', but decided those words were too silly to go with a beautiful tune. *Yesterday* is now the most covered popular song of all time – over 3,000 versions had been recorded at the last count.

TV footage

Footage of the September 11, 2001 attacks on New York is shown more often on television than any other recent news event. But pictures of Neil Armstrong's 1969 walk on the moon is still the most requested archive footage at ITN, whose newsreels date back to 1896. In an article published in the *Independent*, Alwyn Lindsey, managing director of their archives, said that the the key to memorable television moments is a combination of visual impact and historical significance. He believes footage of September 11 will overtake Armstrong on the moon as the most requested archive footage ever.

Most requested archive footage (ITN, Reuters, Channel Four, British Pathe)
1 Neil Armstrong's moonwalk, 1969
2 The assassination of John F. Kennedy, 1963
3 The funeral of Diana, Princess of Wales, 1997
4 Bobby Moore lifting the World Cup, 1966
5 The SAS storming of the Iranian embassy in London, 1980
6 Margaret Thatcher's tearful departure from 10 Downing Street, 1990
7 Neville Chamberlain's 'Peace for our time' speech, 1938
8 Hindenburg disaster, 1937
9 Atomic blasts at Hiroshima and Nagasaki, 1945

Most complained-about advertisements

Every year in the UK hundreds of people contact the Advertising Standards Authority (ASA) to complain about an advertisement that has offended or upset them. Yet one of the most complained-about ads in 2003 was also voted one of the best in the industry.

An advertising campaign by Barnardo's, the children's charity, was banned by the ASA for its use of 'shocking images'. One ad showed a huge, computer-generated cockroach emerging from the mouth of a newborn baby. Barnardo's said the ads 'caused distress for good reason', just like road safety advertisements. But 466 people registered a complaint and the ASA ruled that the campaign could 'cause serious or widespread offence'.

Shortly afterwards, *Campaign* magazine voted the Barnardo's campaign number 6 in its Top 10 for 2003.

SOME OF THE MOST COMPLAINED-ABOUT
ADVERTISEMENTS BETWEEN 1995–2003

1 British Safety Council advertisement aimed at raising awareness for National Condom Week, 1995. A leaflet featuring Pope John Paul II wearing a safety helmet above the text: 'Thou shalt always wear a condom.'
    1187 complaints, which were upheld.

2 Yves Saint Laurent poster for a perfume, showing a naked woman lying on her back, 2000. Complainants said the image was degrading to women, the advertisers said it was a 'work of art'.
    948 complaints, which were upheld.

3 A.G. Barr poster advertising Irn Bru, 1998. The poster featured a cow next to the text: 'When I'm a burger, I want to be washed down with Irn Bru.'
    589 complaints, not upheld.

4 Club 18–30 series of advertisements, 1995. The posters and press advertisements featured headlines such as: 'You get two weeks for being drunk and disorderly', 'It's not all sex, sex, sex. There's a bit of sun and sea as well', and 'Girls, can we interest you in a package holiday?' above a photograph of a man with a prominent bulge in his boxer shorts. Complainants said the posters were obscene, irresponsible and offensive. The advertisers said they reflected the essence of the holidays through humour and colloquialisms.
    490 complaints, which were upheld.

5 Gossard poster for underwear, 1996. The posters were headed: 'WHO SAID A WOMAN CAN'T GET PLEASURE FROM SOMETHING SOFT' next to a woman in her underwear lying on the grass.
    321 complaints, not upheld.

UK's top crime writers

Crime is the most popular book genre in the UK, second only to general fiction, with more than 3 million crime and mystery paperbacks sold in 2003. The crime market is dominated by a handful of writers, with just ten authors accounting for almost half of all sales.

THE UK'S TOP 10

	Author	No. of books	Value £
1	John Grisham	17	4,142,782
2	Ian Rankin	37	1,740,368
3	Kathy Reichs	16	1,599,250
4	Martina Cole	14	1,495,676
5	Michael Connelly	30	1,406,013
6	James Patterson	26	1,390,015
7	Patterson/Gross	4	1,172,507
8	Jeffery Deaver	24	1,066,338
9	Harlan Coben	20	1,034,289
10	Lee Child	12	907,798

Source: survey carried out for The Bookseller *magazine*

Great *Guardian* corrections

UK newspaper the *Guardian* used to be well known for typographical mistakes, much to the amusement of all other papers. My favourite is from September 11, 1986, on the Sports pages about a Scotland football game. I still have it pinned on my wall:

'One day the great manager and the great team will arrive and the blue shits will assume their rightful place on top of the world.'

Since then, modern technology has greatly reduced such printing errors, but *The Guardian* now makes a great virtue of each week correcting any factual, grammatical or stylistic mistakes their writers may make.

On January 3, 2004, looking back at the previous year, they printed a selection of that year's more interesting corrections and clarifications:

> Interview with Sir Jack Hayward, chair of Wolverhampton Wanderers: 'Our team was the worst in the First Division and I'm sure it'll be the worst in the Premier League.'
>
> Sir Jack had just declined the offer of a hot drink, and what he actually said was: 'Our tea was the worst in the First Division and I'm sure it'll be the worst in the Premier League.'

> St Andrews University does not sport an apostrophe, and nor does the town of the same name.

> A picture of the Queen was flipped, making her appear to be left-handed.

> A report about 19th-century Lowther Castle said Boswell, Hogarth and Pitt had visited. Boswell died in 1795, Hogarth in 1764, Pitt the Elder in 1778 and Pitt the Younger in 1806.

> In an article on health and clothing, the optimum temperature of testicles was given as 22 degrees Celsius below core body temperature (instead of 2.2 degrees).

Most stolen artists

Stealing a famous painting by a famous artist seems a pretty potty thing to do. For a start, how can you sell it? Even if you put it on your own wall, someone might recognise it. But there have always been unprincipled millionaires, with very secure walls in very secure, well-hidden mansions, willing to ogle their favourite artist in total privacy. And, of course, there's the insurance. Having stolen the painting, keep it hidden for a while, then do a secret deal with the insurance firms.

In recent years, another reason has emerged for nicking a masterpiece – keeping it as a Get out of Jail Free Card. The Art and Artists Unit of the Metropolitan Police now believe that many professional thieves steal famous works of art and stash them away, then when they get caught for some other crime say, 'Psst, wanna know where a £20 million Picasso is hidden?' They then attempt to decrease their sentence by supplying the information.

Whatever the reasons, stealing masterpieces is on the increase. The Art Loss Register, a London-based company, holds records of 140,000 paintings stolen from all around the world. And they have kindly revealed the Top 10 most popular artists considered worth running away with...

Top 10	Artist	Number of works stolen
1	Pablo Picasso	551
2	Joan Miró	356
3	Marc Chagall	309
4	Salvador Dali	231
5	Pierre-Auguste Renoir	209
6	Albrecht Dürer	203
7	Rembrandt van Rijn	174
8	Andy Warhol	159
9	David Teniers	127
10	Henri Matisse	108

Source: Art Loss Register

Starting young

E famous

Backstage demands

Blue plaques

People who snubbed
the Queen

Royal engagements

Prime Ministers
who were adulterers

Starting old

Burial places of
the famous

CELEBRITIES

Starting young

Here's a list of some interesting and also some awful events that happened to people when they were very, very young.

Aged 1: Charles Lindbergh III, son of the famous American aviator Colonel Lindbergh, was kidnapped. A ransom was paid, but the baby was later found dead.

Aged 2: Princess Anne began riding lessons. They were not wasted, for she later rode for Britain in the Olympics and in 1971 was voted BBC Sportswoman of the Year.

Aged 3: Elizabeth Taylor gave her first Royal Command Performance – dancing with her ballet class before the King and Queen in 1935.

Aged 4: Malcolm X, the African-American activist leader, saw his family home burned down by the Klu Klux Klan.

Aged 5: The Dalai Lama was enthroned as spiritual and temporal leader of Tibet, in 1940. He was later forced to flee by Chinese communists.

Aged 6: Wolfgang Amadeus Mozart was writing minuets and touring the courts of Europe, giving recitals on the violin.

Aged 7: Thomas Macaulay, British historian, who had learned to read aged 3, started compiling a history of the world.

Aged 8: Charlie Chaplin appeared on stage in a clog-dancing routine called 'Eight Lancashire Lads'.

Aged 9: Lord Byron was supposedly introduced to sex by his family nurse, an otherwise devout Scottish girl, who crept into his bed and 'aroused him sexually'. She also allowed him to watch her making love.

Aged 10: Louis XVII of France died. His father, Louis XVI, and mother were guillotined during the French Revolution. The surviving French nobles declared young Louis the next king, but aged 8 he was imprisoned and died two years later.

First jobs of the famous

Or at least jobs they had in their early years, before they became famous for what they became famous for. In showbusiness it's pretty normal to have a variety of jobs before making it, but it can also happen in other professions and careers.

Warren Beatty – rat catcher
Bruce Willis – lorry driver
Michael Douglas – petrol pump attendant
Michael Caine – Smithfield meat market porter
Steve McQueen – towel boy in brothel
Jack Nicholson – mail room boy at MGM
Glenda Jackson – shop assistant at Boots the Chemist
Raquel Welch – secretary to a bishop
Sean Connery – milkman
Sylvester Stallone – beautician
Roger Moore – male model for knitting patterns
Marilyn Monroe – aircraft factory worker
Jeremy Irons – busker
Tom Cruise – gardener
Bob Hoskins – sailor in Norwegian merchant navy
Mick Jagger – porter in a mental hospital
Sting – clerk in Inland Revenue
Annie Lennox – fish factory worker
Cilla Black – hairdresser
Ozzy Osbourne – slaughterhouse labourer
Elton John – messenger boy for music publisher
Kylie Minogue – shop assistant

Paul McCartney – electrical coil winder
Tom Jones – apprentice glove cutter
Julio Iglesias – goalkeeper at Real Madrid (youth team)
Dame Kiri te Kanawa – telephone operator
Dame Shirley Bassey – chamberpot factory worker
Rod Stewart – grave digger
Phil Collins – painter and decorator
Madonna – waitress at burger bar
Jasper Carrott – travelling denture paste salesman
Dawn French – teacher
Billy Connolly – welder
Julie Walters – nurse
David Jason – garage mechanic

Abraham Lincoln – postman
George Bush Snr – equipment clerk
John Major – builder's labourer
Ken Livingstone – lab. technician
Hitler – designer of advertising posters for deodorants
Mussolini – chocolate factory worker
Alexander Fleming – shipping clerk
Pope John Paul II – quarry labourer
Tchaikovsky – office clerk
Gaugin – stockbroker's agent
Van Gogh – schoolteacher in Ramsgate
Charles Dickens – shoe polish factory worker
Mark Twain – apprentice printer
Robert Louis Stevenson – lawyer
Somerset Maugham – doctor
Thomas Hardy – architect
Walt Disney – apple masher in jelly factory
Diana, Princess of Wales – children's nanny
Socrates – stone worker

Backstage demands

Music stars often have very specific requirements for their dressing rooms – as outlined in their contracts. They cover obvious professional requirements such as stage design, sound systems and lighting, but very often include the artist's own personal demands.

U2 Zoo TV Tour, 1992
1 case Rolling Rock or a local domestic bottled beer
4 cases Heineken
½ case Guinness Stout
1 x 5th Cuervo Tequila
1 x 5th Stolli or Absolut Vodka
1 x 5th Jack Daniel's Black
2 x 5ths Moet White Star Champagne
3 very good French white Chardonnay
3 very good French red Bordeaux
2 Mouton Cadet red wines
2 Jacobs Creek or Black Opal Australian white wine
1 medium-quality Port or Sherry

Sting's dressing room, 2000 Tour, North American leg
6 large bath-size towels and two bars of soap
Carpeted
Low-key lighting
2-seater couch
2 armchairs
A table for catering requirements
2 coffee tables
2 large bottles Evian Water (on ice)
2 large bottles Evian Water (room temperature)
1 bottle full-bodied red wine
Hot tea
Kettle

Teapot
Cups
Saucers
12 fresh lemons
1 jar of honey
Fresh, skinned and grated ginger root

Back Street Boys catering requirements
All meals must be prepared in-house
No take-out meals or fast food will be accepted
All meals are to be sit-down meals with clean tablecloths,
real plates (no paper), silverware, real coffee cups

Deli tray and bread:
Available throughout the day
Sandwich meat
Cheese
Crackers & chips
Butter, mustard, mayo etc.
Assorted breads
A bowl of fruit

Large bowl of soup:
To be out at 3.30 each day for the arrival of the artist

Breakfast:
To be served at a time determined by at load in
Eggs
Bacon
Sausage
Assortment of cold cereal
Assorted breads
Jelly
Peanut butter
Fresh fruit
Yogurt in assorted flavours

Lunch:
To be served around 12.00 noon
Hot sandwiches
Hamburgers
French dip
Hot turkey
Sloppy Joe's
Tacos
2 types of salad
I type of soup
Condiments as needed

Dinner:
To be served no less than 2 hours
before BSB on stage
1 chicken dish
1 beef dish
1 vegetarian or fish dish
2 side dishes
Cooked vegetables
Potatoes
Rice
Beans

P. Diddy catering requirements
1 A catering representative must be present at all times
2 Before serving, all food and ice must be inspected for hair, package, paper etc. and all catering staff must wear hairnets
3 All drinks should be iced down 20 minutes prior to serving in large trash containers lined with plastic bags
4 Total number of towels needed for day of the show:
nine dozen bath-size towels (Crew)
eight dozen hand-size towels (Artist)
20 bars of soap for showers
5 Please try to avoid the frying of food in daily meals

unless it is necessary and include low-fat cooking products and condiments
6 All juices in dressing rooms should be in boxes unless otherwise specified

**Luciano Pavarotti,
miscellaneous requirements**
There must be no distinct smells anywhere near the Artist
There cannot be any flowers located backstage in the dressing room, or around the stage
There is to be no smoking backstage, nor is there to be any noise

Kenny G's dressing room requirements
Large, clean floor carpet
Nice fresh flower arrangement with Japanese flair
2 x 8 foot tables with tablecloths and skirts
2 lamps
2 chairs
2 tables
Closet or clothes rack with hangers
AC outlets
Mirror
Soap
12 towels
Shower and lavatory facilities with access to only Kenny G

Kenny G's chef's room:
Running hot and cold water
2 x 8 foot tables
3 bath tubs
4 x 110w outlets
12 complete meal flatware setups
Silverwear
No plastic
No styrofoam

12 x 8 ounce glasses
Cloth napkins
4 quart chaffing dish with sterno and serving utensils
1 whisk
Mixing bowl

Source: www.thesmokinggun.com

Blue plaques

The first plaque erected by the Royal Society of Arts was on Lord Byron's London home in 1867. Thirty-six plaques later, the London County Council took over the job, followed in 1965 by the Greater London Council and then English Heritage in 1986. In recent years plaques have been erected in other English cities – first Merseyside, then Birmingham, Portsmouth and Southampton. Today there are nearly 800 plaques in London.

Candidates are only eligible for a plaque either 100 years after their birth, or 20 years after their death. English Heritage now erects around 20 blue plaques a year.

Latest blue plaques

January 2004
Private Frederick Hitch,
hero of Rorke's Drift

October 2003
William Petty,
'the Jesuit of Berkeley Square'

November 2003
Lao She,
revered Chinese writer

October 2003
William Roberts, RA,
distinctive and respected artist

November 2003
Henry Hall,
legendary dance band leader

October 2003
Mary Shelley, author of
Frankenstein

Source: English Heritage

People who snubbed the Queen

In 2003 a secret file was leaked to the press listing 300 singers, actors, writers and TV stars who had refused an honour from Queen Elizabeth II. Reasons for the refusal – offered by prime ministers on behalf of the Queen – were not given.

J.G. Ballard	Trevor Howard
Honor Blackman	Aldous Huxley
David Bowie	Philip Larkin
John le Carré	Nigella Lawson
Roald Dahl	L.S. Lowry
Albert Finney	George Melly
Dawn French	Anthony Powell
Robert Graves	J.B. Priestley
Graham Green	Jennifer Saunders
Alfred Hitchcock	Alastair Sim
David Hockney	Evelyn Waugh

Royal engagements

The Prince of Wales leads the Royal pack when it comes to attending official engagements in the UK, but it is the Duke of York who has the most engagements overseas – and the Duke of Edinburgh who attends the most dinners.

The following list, based on the Court Circular for 2003, was compiled by Mr Tim O'Donovan in a letter written to *The Times*. O'Donovan points out that, in spite of advancing years, the Queen still has a hectic workload. He emphasises that the figures shouldn't be converted into a league table of Royal performance since some engagements – and their preparation – take longer than others.

	A	B	C	D	E
The Queen	154	75	233	462	16
Duke of Edinburgh	216	167	44	427	29
Prince of Wales	251	109	134	494	110
Duke of York	198	70	28	296	179
Earl of Wessex	189	55	24	268	144
Countess of Wessex	125	36	13	174	5
Princess Royal	293	93	69	455	169
Duke of Gloucester	139	39	29	207	21
Duchess of Gloucester	105	30	14	149	12
Duke of Kent	147	34	22	203	14
Princess Alexander	90	35	25	150	26

A Official visits, opening ceremonies and other engagements
B Receptions, lunches, dinners and banquets
C Other engagements, including investitures, meetings attended and audiences given
D Total number of engagements in UK
E Total number of engagements on official overseas tours

Prime ministers who were adulterers

Gladstone is said to have maintained that he knew eleven prime ministers in his lifetime, seven of whom were adulterers, though not necessarily while they were in office. It's a list that is hard to assemble, at least with complete certainty, as several of the allegations have still never been properly documented. (There are rumours about Gladstone himself, and the prostitutes he 'befriended'.)

The following list was checked with the late A.J.P. Taylor, who said that in each case there is either reasonable proof, such as a court case (certain), or contemporary reports that strongly suggest at least one adulterous affair (probable).

Since he helped to compile it, we have been able to add another name to the list, thanks to the good work of Edwina Currie.

Duke of Devonshire (certain)
Lord John Russell (certain)
Duke of Wellington (certain)
George Canning (probable)
Lord Grey (certain)
Lord Melbourne (probable)
Lord Aberdeen (probable)
Lord Palmerston (certain)
Benjamin Disraeli (certain)
David Lloyd George (certain)
Herbert Asquith, Earl of Oxford (probable)
John Major (certain)

Starting old

Here's a list of some startling achievements by people during their supposed later and declining years.

Aged 70: Alfred Wallis, Cornish primitive artist, first started to paint. Until then he had been a cabin boy, fisherman and rag-and-bone man, till he retired. When his wife died, he started to paint marine scenes. St Ives' artist Ben Nicholson saw them and made Wallis' work known worldwide.

Aged 71: Leni Riefenstal, Hitler's favourite documentary film-maker, took up scuba diving, lying about her age and saying she was only 51.

Aged 72: The Marquis de Sade acquired his last mistress. He persuaded her to shave off her pubic hair for him. He died two years later, in 1841.

Aged 73: Konrad Adenauer became Chancellor of Germany, in 1949, remaining in office until 1963.

Aged 76: John XXII became Pope, in 1958, but lasted only five years.

Aged 77: Clara Barton, founder of the American Red Cross, went off to serve in Cuba during the Spanish-American war of 1898.

Aged 78: Sir Thomas Beecham, the conductor, set off on an international tour with the Royal Philharmonic Orchestra.

Aged 79: Dame Edith Evans, English actress, won the New York Critics Award in 1967 for her performance in *The Whisperers*.

Aged 80: George Burns, American comedian, won an Oscar for *The Sunshine Boys*, in 1976, becoming the oldest person to win an Oscar.

Aged 81: Benjamin Franklin, statesman and scientist, helped to frame the American constitution, in 1787.

Aged 82: Winston Churchill published the first part of his four-volume work, *A History of the English-Speaking Peoples*. He had recently given up the post of prime minister, in 1955 aged 80, but remained as an MP for another ten years.

Aged 83: Agatha Christie celebrated in 1974 the fact that her play *The Mousetrap*, which had opened in 1952, had established the record for the world's longest-running play in the same theatre. Even then it didn't close, but moved down the road to another theatre.

Aged 84: Claude Monet completed one of his greatest works, a series of murals for the orangery beside his water lily pond at Giverny, France.

Aged 85: Coco Chanel, still running her fashion empire, had a musical based on her life open on Broadway, with Katharine Hepburn in the leading role.

Aged 86: Elizabeth Blackwell, the first woman to qualify as a doctor in the USA, was in 1907 still practising as a gynaecologist.

Aged 87: Bernard Berenson, American art critic and collector, completed the third part of his autobiography.

Aged 88: Pablo Casals, the great Spanish cellist, continued to give concerts around the world.

Aged 89: Albert Schweitzer, French missionary doctor, was still in charge of the hospital he had established in Gabon, West Africa.

Aged 90: Margaret Murray, British archaeologist, became president of the English Folklore Society. She was writing books until she was 100.

Aged 91: Eamon de Valera was still president of the Irish Republic, but retired the same year and died two years later.

Aged 92: Fenner Brockway, Labour MP and peace campaigner, published his book *Britain's First Socialists*.

Aged 93: William Dubois, American historian and leading figure in the National Association for the Advancement of Coloured People, converted to communism.

Aged 94: Bertrand Russell, English philosopher, was still active as an anti-war and nuclear arms campaigner.

Aged 95: Arthur Rubenstein, pianist, gave his last public concert, the oldest-known age for any virtuoso concert performer.

Aged 96: Grandma Moses, already enormously successful in the USA, gave her first exhibition of paintings in London.

Aged 97: Winifred Rushforth, Scottish doctor and psychoanalyst, was still conducting dream therapy groups in Edinburgh.

Aged 98: Fred Streeter, English broadcaster and gardener, was still answering hundreds of thousands of gardening letters.

Aged 99: Dora Booth, a major in the Salvation Army and granddaughter of General Booth, took part in a TV talk show with Russell Harty. When asked if, had her grandfather been alive, he would have come on TV, she replied, 'No, he would have been doing something more important.'

Aged 100: Estelle Winwood, English-born actress who appeared in 40 Broadway plays and many films, was living in California, smoking 60 cigarettes a day, drinking sherry and playing bridge most evenings. She had been married four times. At 100 she said she was 'still waiting for something wonderful to happen'.

Source: Book of Ages, Desmond Morris, 1983

Burial places of the famous

Many of the great and the good in British history have ended up at Westminster Abbey, but quite a few managed to leave their bones or ashes elsewhere.

Queen Boudicea of the Iceni, died 61AD: under platform 10, King's Cross Station, London. Probably true – she was killed in battle by the Romans on the site of what is now the station.

King Arthur: under the ruins of Glastonbury Abbey, allegedly.

The Venerable Bede: Durham Cathedral. Definitely.

King Canute: Winchester Cathedral.

William the Conqueror: St Stephen's Church, Caen, Normandy.

Henry VIII: St George's Chapel, Windsor Castle, Berks, beside his third wife, Jane Seymour.

Samuel Pepys: St Olave's Church, Hart Street, City of London, alongside his wife, Elizabeth.

Queen Victoria: Royal Mausoleum, Frogmore, Windsor, Berks.

Napoleon III, Emperor of the French: Abbey Church, St Michael, Farnborough, Hampshire.

Benjamin Disraeli: St Michael's Churchyard, Hughenden, Bucks.

Winston Churchill: St Martin's Churchyard, Bladon, Oxfordshire.

Horatio Nelson: St Paul's Cathedral, London.

Jeremy Bentham, philosopher and social reformer: University College, London, where his embalmed body is kept in a showcase.

Karl Marx: Highgate New Cemetery, London.

Michael Faraday: Highgate Old Cemetery, London.

George Stephenson: Trinity Church, Chesterfield, Derbyshire.

Shakespeare: Holy Trinity Church, Stratford-upon-Avon.

Jane Austen: Winchester Cathedral.

Mrs Beeton: Norwood Cemetery, London.

Samuel Taylor Coleridge: St Michael's Church, Highgate, London.
Sir Arthur Conan Doyle: All Saints Churchyard, Minstead, Hampshire.

Lewis Carroll: Guildford Cemetery, Surrey.

Charlotte Brontë: St Michael and All Angels Church, Haworth, Yorkshire; also sister Emily. Anne is buried at St Mary's Churchyard, Castle Road, Scarborough.

T.S. Eliot: St Michael's Church, East Coker, Somerset.

D.H. Lawrence: Eastwood Cemetery, Notts.

George Orwell: All Saints, Sutton Courtney, Oxon.

John Ruskin: St Andrew's Churchyard, Coniston, Cumbria.

Percy Bysshe Shelley: St Peter's Churchyard, Bournemouth, Dorset, where his heart was re-interred after his death by drowning in Italy.

Virginia Woolf: Monks House, Rodmell, Sussex, where her ashes were buried in the garden.

Beatrix Potter: Near Sawrey, Cumbria. Her ashes were scattered in a field by her shepherd and the exact location was never revealed.

Forence Nightingale: St Margaret's Churchyard, East Wellow, Hampshire. Only her initials, F.N., appear on her tombstone.

Source: Who's buried where in England, *a Constable guide, 1982*

FOOD
AND
DRINK

Food quotations

Tell me what you eat, and I will tell you what you are.
ANTHELME BRILLAT-SAVARIN (1755–1826),
The Physiology of Taste, 1825

*The most remarkable thing about my mother is that for
30 years she served the family nothing but leftovers.
The original meal has never been found.*
CALVIN TRILLIN (1935–)

He who comes first, eats first.
[Familiar as: *First come first served.*]
EIKE VON REPKOW (~1220), *Sachsenspiegel*

*Preach not to others what they should eat, but eat as
becomes you, and be silent.*
EPICTETUS (55AD–135AD)

Food is an important part of a balanced diet.
FRAN LEBOWITZ (1950–)

*What some call health, if purchased by perpetual anxiety
about diet, isn't much better than tedious disease.*
GEORGE DENNISON PRENTICE (1802–1870)

*Part of the secret of success in life is to eat what you like
and let the food fight it out inside.*
MARK TWAIN (1835–1910)

Never eat more than you can lift.
MISS PIGGY

*Ask not what you can do for your country.
Ask what's for lunch.*
ORSON WELLES (1915–1985)

*There are people who strictly deprive themselves of each
and every eatable, drinkable, and smokable which has
in any way acquired a shady reputation. They pay
this price for health. And health is all they get for it.
How strange it is. It is like paying out your whole
fortune for a cow that has gone dry.*
MARK TWAIN (1835–1910)

*Fish is the only food that is considered spoiled
once it smells like what it is.*
P. J. O'ROURKE (1947–)

You can tell a lot about a fellow's character
by his way of eating jellybeans.
RONALD REAGAN (1911–),
quoted in *The Observer*, March 29, 1981

*I've been on a diet for two weeks
and all I've lost is two weeks.*
TOTIE FIELDS (1930–1978)

Source: www.quotationspage.com

Great food inventions

Here's a list of foods we take for granted, and who invented them.

Croissant

The French are generally credited with re-inventing the
croissant dough in its current form, especially as it's a French
word meaning crescent or crescent-shaped, and the first recipes
appeared in the early 20th century. But, according to one legend,
a Polish soldier invented the croissant in 1683 in Vienna, during
the war between Austria and Turkey.

Frozen foods

Lovers of frozen foods can thank an American taxidermist, Clarence Birdseye from Brooklyn, New York, for them. Having seen people in the Arctic preserving fresh fish and meat in barrels of seawater, which became quickly frozen, Birdseye realised that rapid freezing meant food would still be fresh when it was later thawed and cooked. In 1923 he spent 7 dollars on an electric fan, buckets of brine and cakes of ice. Six years later he sold his patents and trademarks for 22 million dollars. Quick frozen foods first went on sale in 1930, in Massachusetts.

Hamburger

Who exactly invented the hamburger – and when – is still up for debate. German immigrants probably brought the hamburger patty to the United States in the 19th century, but as for inventing the hamburger – some say it was 15-year-old Charles Nagreen in 1885 at a county fair in Wisconsin, others that it was Frank Menches in 1892 at a county fair in Ohio. Either way, it would be a good few decades before the trademark for the name 'cheeseburger' was awarded, to Louis Ballast of the Humpty Dumpty Drive-In, Denver, Colorado in 1935. Meanwhile, the slugburger – a deep fat-fried beef mixture – has its very own annual festival in Mississippi each July.

Hot dogs

Again, the origins can be traced back to German immigrants, who introduced the wienerwurst, or wiener, to the United States. But it was a catering director at New York City's Polo grounds who put the hot dog into a bun – although some say the inventor was Charles Feltman at Coney Island amusement park. As for where the term hot dog came from, some attribute it to a 19th-century American sports cartoonist who caricatured Germans as dachshund dogs. His cartoons alleged that cheap wieners sold at Coney Island had dog meat, and in 1913 the term 'hot dog' was officially banned from signs on the Island. The term first appeared in print in 1900.

HP Sauce

This was apparently created by a chef at the British Houses of Parliament, hence its name, but the recipe was invented by a Nottingham shopkeeper who traded it with a vinegar company in order to settle a debt. It's also known as 'Wilson's Gravy', after Harold Wilson, Labour Prime Minister of the 1960s and 1970s, who was said to cover his food with HP Sauce.

Ice-cream cone

Italo Marchiony, an Italian who immigrated to New York City in the 1800s, was granted a patent for the ice cream cone in 1903 – he claimed he had created the cone in 1896. But cones were also independently introduced at the 1904 St Louis World's Fair, where they were sold for the first time, and many credit Charles Menches with the invention. When Menches ran out of ice cream dishes he borrowed the cone idea from another stallholder, Ernest Hamwi, a Syrian who was selling Zalabia, a Middle Eastern wafer-like pastry. However, there were 50 other ice-cream vendors at the fair, and several also claimed the invention for themselves.

Iced tea

Invented by Richard Blechyden, an Englishman selling beverages at the St Louis World's Fair in 1904.

Instant mashed potatoes

Invented by a Canadian, Edward A. Asselbergs, in 1962.

Marmite

A German chemist first found that spent brewer's yeast could be made into a concentrated food product, but it wasn't until 1902 that a British company managed to manufacture the yeast extract for commercial purposes. The Marmite Food Company initially rented a disused malt house in Burton-on-Trent and later extended operations to London. Marmite's popularity was boosted in 1912 with the discovery of vitamins – the yeast in

Marmite providing a good source of vitamin B. Marmite was served to British soldiers during both world wars.

Pasta

Pasta might be regarded as the all-Italian food, but it originated in China around 40 centuries ago, and wasn't introduced to Italy until 1291AD. The first documented recipe for pasta was in a Sicilian cookery book in 1000. In the 1800s pasta began to be combined with tomato-based sauces, and a variety of new shapes took off. 'Lasagna' (lasagne) may come from the Greek 'lasanon', meaning a chamber pot.

Pizza

The invention of modern pizza is often attributed to a Naples baker in the 1800s, but an earlier form of pizza had been eaten for centuries in many Mediterranean countries. The earliest pizza shop was reportedly opened in 1830 in Naples, while the first pizzeria in North America was opened in New York City in 1905.

Popcorn

Popcorn maize goes back a very long way. In 1948 two American scientists discovered ears of popcorn in a cave in New Mexico, which were carbon dated to be about 5,600 years old. Ancient popcorn poppers have also been found in Peru, dating back to pre-Inca times.

In the 16th century popcorn was an important food for the Aztec Indians, and in the 17th century Native Americans reportedly brought popcorn with them to meetings with English colonists. The first machine to pop popcorn was invented in Chicago in 1885, and the first brand name popcorn in the USA, named Jolly Time, was launched in 1914. Popcorn saw a rise in popularity with the opening of movie theatres in the early 20th century and again when television took off in the 1950s.

Powdered milk

The Mongolians are said to be the first to have produced powdered milk, back in the 13th century. They added millet and ice to milk, boiled it until it thickened and then let it dry.

Sandwich

Invented by Englishman John Montagu, the Earl of Sandwich, who wanted a meal that could be eaten with one hand so that he wouldn't have to interrupt his gambling at cards.

Tomato ketchup

'Ketchup' originally comes from the Chinese 'ke-stiap', a pickled fish sauce. F. & J. Heinz Company began selling tomato ketchup in 1876.

Vegemite

A yeast product similar to Marmite. The spread was invented by an Australian scientist and, after a national competition to find a name, was launched in 1923. During the Second World War both military and civilian populations had Vegemite in their rations. In 1935 the recipe and manufacturing methods were sold to the American company Kraft Foods. Nowadays, nine out of ten Australian households have a jar of Vegemite in the pantry.

Sources:
www.thinkquest.org
www.globalgourmet.com
www.inventors.about.com
www.lapiazzaonline.com
www.homecooking.about.com
www.ilovemarmite.com
www.danielroy.tripod.com
www.whatscookingamerica.net

Top diets in the USA

Internet searches for the perfect diet are popular all the year round, but especially just after New Year, according to the Internet search engine Lycos. It ranks the following diets and diet products as its Top 10 for 2002. Big name diets like Weight Watchers came top in the United States, but in Canada a popular search was for 'apple cider vinegar', since pills made from the vinegar allegedly promote weight loss.

1 Weight Watchers	6 Body for Life
2 Atkins Diet	7 Richard Simmons
3 Metabolife	8 Hollywood Diet
4 Zone Diet	9 Jenny Craig
5 Mayo Clinic Diet	10 Slim Fast

Household food bills

The British household today spends less of its weekly expenditure on milk and sugar than it did 20 years ago, but more on fresh fruit, fish and alcohol – in 1992 (when figures on alcohol spending were first assessed) the average spent per person was 43 pence, in 2000 it was £1.50.

	Pence per person per week		
Selected items	*1980*	*1990*	*2000*
Liquid whole milk	67.5	61.9	31.3
All carcase meat	110.8	121.7	110.7
Fish	32.1	66.6	80.2
Sugar	11.6	11.1	6.6
Fresh green vegetables	10.3	22.0	35.0
Fresh fruit	28.0	65.1	95.0
Bread	44.2	68.6	73.0
Total weekly expenditure on all foods	£7.21	£12.12	£15.20

Source: National Food Survey, MAFF

Consumer concerns

Barely a month goes by without one food hazard warning or another –
whether salmonella, dye contamination or donkey meat in salami. But
while UK consumers remain worried about GM foods, they are far less
worried than they used to be about BSE.

Concern	2000	2003
BSE	61%	42%
Raw meat	70%	63%
Eggs	26%	20%
GM foods	43%	38%

Consumers also seem a lot more educated, with 78% claiming to check
food labels:

	2000	2003
Aware we should eat 5 portions of fruit and vegetables a day	43%	59%
Actually eat the 5 portions	26%	28%
Look for total salt content in a product	22%	36%

Shopping and eating habits
50% of consumers shop about once a week
95% shop at supermarkets
6 out of 10 enjoy cooking
⅖ths cook meals from raw or fresh ingredients once a day
50% sit down once a day for their main meal
with household members

Source: Food Standards Agency
Consumer Attitudes to Food Survey

Fish and chips

Chips are Britain's favourite food – but where did the great British fish and chip trade come from? Well, the chips part came from the 18th-century French invention *pommes frites*. The fish part goes back to early 19th-century 'fried fish warehouses', as described in Charles Dickens' novel *Oliver Twist*. The fish was sold by street vendors, and the accompaniment was usually bread. In the 1860s fish was finally teamed with chips, creating a tasty and affordable meal.

Over the course of the next 100 years, fish and chips became not only a national institution, but a vital source of nutrition for families – helping to fuel the workforce of the industrial revolution. Fish and chips became so essential to the diet of the ordinary man and woman that one shop in Bradford had to employ a doorman to control the queue at busy times during 1931. There are now around 8,500 fish and chip shops across the UK – that's eight for every one McDonald's outlet.

Fish and chip facts

The first fish and chip shop in the north of England opened in Mossely, near Oldham, Lancashire, around 1863. It had the following inscription in the window: 'This is the first fish and chip shop in the world.' But in London, Joseph Malin had already opened a fish and chip shop in Cleveland Street in 1860.

In the 1930s the Territorial Army prepared for battle on fish and chips provided in special catering tents erected at training camps.

During the Second World War,

Lord Woolton, Minister of Food, declared that fish and chips was among the few foods not to be rationed.

In *The Victor Book for Boys*, 1960s comic hero Alf Tupper relied on a 'sixpennyworth' of fish and chips to help him break the world record for the mile.

Sean Connery is the man most women would like to see serving them fish and chips – chosen by 26% of women respondents – while Catherine Zeta-Jones came out top among men.

A survey showed that nine out of ten women say a man should have basic cooking skills – and fish was chosen by one-third of women as the dish most likely to put them in the mood for seduction.

In 2000 nearly 300 million fish and chip shop meals were sold throughout the UK – that's six servings for every man, woman and child in the country.

The record for the largest number of portions sold in one day by an independent fish and chip shop is 4,000.

Seventy per cent of the UK population eats fish and chips at least once every six months.

Britain produces 350,000 tonnes of frozen chips a year.
Two million tonnes of British potatoes (30% of the national potato crop) are made into chips each year.

Northerners are most likely to fry their chips at home (28% claim they cook them from scratch).

Cod and chips is the nation's favourite takeaway (41%), followed by chicken tikka masala and pilau rice (21%).

Maris Piper is the chip shops' favourite potato variety, used by 98% of chip shops.

*Sources: Federation of Fish Friers, The British Potato Council,
www.bulford-fish-and-chips.co.uk*

Best fish and chip shops

A third of the UK population believes that Blackpool serves the best fish and chips in the country, according to a MORI survey. But the geographical spread of past Fish and Chip Shop of the Year competition winners shows great fish and chip shops can be found all over the UK.

Brownsover Fish Bar, Rugby – 2003
Allports, Pwllheli – 2001

Les Manning, Cheshire – 2000
Bizzie Lizzies, Skipton, North Yorkshire – 1999
Zanre's, Peterhead, Scotland – 1998
Bervie Chipper, Inverbervie, Scotland – 1997
The Halfway Fish Bar, Poole, Dorset – 1996
Hutchinsons, Helston, Cornwall – 1995
The West End Cafe, Rothesay, Isle of Bute, Scotland – 1994
Reed Square Fish Bar, Erdington, Birmingham – 1993
Elite Fish Bar, Ruskington, Lincolnshire – 1992
Chez Fred, Westbourne, Bournemouth – 1991
The Ashvale Fish Restaurant, Aberdeen – 1990
Skippers Fish and Chips, Peterborough – 1989
Toffs, Muswell Hill, London – 1988

Source: Federation of Fish Friers

Wrapping rage

Each year in the UK 67,000 people injure themselves while trying to do something as apparently simple as open a can of beans or unwrap a sandwich.

The 10 worst things to open

Tops of bleach bottles
and lavatory cleaners

Shrink-wrapped cheese and ham

Sealed sandwich packages

Ring-pull cans

Tins of meat and fish

Milk and juice cartons

Childproof tops
on medicine bottles

Cellophane tops
on microwave ready meals

Soap powder boxes

Biscuits

Source: survey conducted for Yours *magazine*

Five food anecdotes

J.M. Barrie was once at a dinner party sitting next to George Bernard Shaw, who was a noted vegetarian. Shaw had requested a special dish of salad and his favourite dressing. When the unpleasant-looking plate of food arrived, Barrie whispered to Shaw, 'Tell me, have you eaten that – or are you going to?'

Handel, the great German composer who lived for many years in England, sent word to a local tavern, booking dinner for two. When he arrived, on his own, the landlord begged his pardon and said he thought that Mr Handel was expecting company. 'I am the company,' said Handel, and ate his way through the dinner for two.

Alfred Hitchcock, the film director, was noted for his fondness for food. At one dinner party he considered the helpings he had been served to be totally inadequate. As Hitchcock was leaving, the host said to him, 'I do hope you will dine with us again soon.' 'By all means,' replied Hitchcock. 'How about now...?'

Eleanor Roosevelt, wife of US President F.D. Roosevelt, was very fond of sweetbreads. In one week they appeared on the White House menu six times. The President eventually wrote a note to his wife: 'I am getting to the point where my stomach rebels and this does not help my relations with foreign ministers. I hit two of them today.'

William Makepeace Thackeray, while on a lecture tour of the USA, was invited to a feast of best American oysters by his US publisher, James T. Fields. He was overcome by the sight of their size and asked how he should devour them. Fields swallowed his in one gulp. Thackeray eventually got up the courage to do the same. Asked how it felt, Thackeray replied, 'As if I had swallowed a baby.'

FOOTBALL

Footballers' Christian names

More footballers called John have won full England caps than with any other popular Christian name – 122 Johns have received the footballing glory. William comes a close second, followed by George, with more traditional names like Arthur and Albert at the bottom of the list. At full international level there has been one Darren (Anderton), but no Deans or Dales. But there has been an Elphinstone (Jackson; one cap, 1891), and an Ephraim (Longworth; five caps between 1920 and 1923) and, of course, Segal Bastard, who won one cap in 1880 against Scotland.

Most popular names of full England internationals

1 John (122)

2 William (80)

3 George (60)

4 Thomas (54)

5 James (53)

6 Robert (42)

7 David (33)

8 Frederick (33)

9 Charles (29)

10 Arthur (28)

Joint 11 Frank (27)

Albert (27)

Source: Sunday Times

Europe's top leagues: 2003

When it comes to the best leagues, attendance-wise, England's Premiership now leads the pack. While Spain might have a couple of individual clubs (Real Madrid and Barcelona) with monster stadia, they also have quite a few clubs lower down La Liga, with modest grounds and a modest following, bringing down their overall average.

TOP 20

No.	Team	Average attendance in top division
1	England	35,318
2	Germany	33,014
3	Spain	28,811
4	Italy	25,667
5	France	19,139
6	Netherlands	15.846
7	Scotland	15,827
8	Russia	11,643
9	Belgium	10,196
10	Sweden	10,161
11	Ukraine	7,584
12	Romania	7,281
13	Portugal	6,844
14	Denmark	6,503
15	Norway	6,201
16	Kazakhstan	5,376
17	Poland	5,350
18	Austria	5,175
19	Czech Republic	4,046
20	Slovakia	3,936

Other English divisions

First Division	15,342
Second Division	7,013
Third Division	4,283

Source: www.european-football-statistics.co.uk

Europe's best-supported clubs: 2003

England likes to think that it not only has the best league, but the best-supported clubs. Alas, our best-supported club, Manchester United, comes only fourth at present in European club ranking, although it boasts that, worldwide, it has more armchair fans and its merchandising sells better than any other club side. And it does have plans to increase its present capacity from 68,000 to 75,000. Note that Arsenal doesn't even make the Top 20, but hold on – it will in 2006–2007 when its new ground opens, taking the maximum attendance up from 38,000 to 60,000.

TOP 20

No.	Team	Average attendance
1	Barcelona (Spain)	72,793
2	Real Madrid (Spain)	69,225
3	Borussia Dortmund (Germany)	68,000
4	Manchester United (England)	67,586
5	Internazionale (Italy)	63,251
6	Milan (Italy)	62,215
7	Schalke 04 (Germany)	60,356
8	Roma (Italy)	58,914
9	Celtic (Scotland)	57,370
10	Bayern Munich (Germany)	52,778
11	Newcastle United (England)	51,373
12	Rangers (Scotland)	48,365
13	Lazio (Italy)	48,051
14	Atletico Madrid (Spain)	46,969
15	Valencia (Spain)	46,250
16	Marseilles (France)	46,173
17	Ajax (Netherlands)	45,041
18	Hamburg (Germany)	43,577
19	Liverpool (England)	43,389
20	Feyenoord (Netherlands)	42,850

Football transfers

It was shock horror in 1905 when Alf Common was transferred from Sunderland to Middlesbrough for £1,000, the first four-figure transfer. Until then, the highest fee had been £400. 'Where will it all end?', so the doom merchants wailed. Could there one day be a £2,000 transfer? Or even, perish the very possibility, a £10,000 transfer? Now read on...

BRITISH TRANSFER RECORDS

Year	Player	From	To	Price
1905	A. Common	Sunderland	Middlesbrough	£1,000
1922	S. Puddefoot	West Ham	Falkirk	£5,000
1922	W. Cresswell	South Shields	Sunderland	£5,500
1928	D. Jack	Bolton	Arsenal	£10,800
1938	B. Jones	Wolves	Arsenal	£14,500
1947	B. Steel	Morton	Derby	£15,000
1947	T. Lawton	Chelsea	Notts Co.	£20,000
1948	L. Shackleton	Newcastle	Sunderland	£20,500
1949	J. Morris	Man. Utd	Derby	£24,000
1949	E. Quigley	Sheff. Wed.	Preston	£26,500
1950	T. Ford	Aston Villa	Sunderland	£30,000
1951	J. Sewell	Notts Co.	Sheff. Wed.	£34,500
1955	E. Firmani	Charlton	Sampdoria	£35,000
1957	J. Charles	Leeds	Juventus	£65,000
1961	D. Law	Man. City	Torino	£100,000
1962	D. Law	Torino	Man. Utd	£115,000
1968	A. Clarke	Fulham	Leicester	£150,000
1969	A. Clarke	Leicester	Leeds	£165,000
1970	M. Peters	West Ham	Tottenham	£200,000
1971	A. Ball	Everton	Arsenal	£220,000
1972	D. Nish	Leicester	Derby	£250,000
1974	B. Latchford	Birmingham	Everton	£350,000
1977	K. Keegan	Liverpool	Hamburg	£500,000
1979	D. Mills	Middlesbrough	West Brom.	£515,000
1979	T. Francis	Birmingham	Nottm Forest	£1.18m
1979	S. Daley	Wolves	Man. City	£1.45m

1979	A. Gray	Aston Villa	Wolves	£1.47m
1981	B. Robson	West Brom.	Man. Utd	£1.5m
1984	R. Wilkins	Man. Utd	Milan	£1.5m
1986	M. Hughes	Man. Utd	Barcelona	£2.3m
1987	I. Rush	Liverpool	Juventus	£3.2m
1989	C. Waddle	Tottenham	Marseilles	£4.3m
1991	D. Platt	Aston Villa	Bari	£5.5m
1992	P. Gascoigne	Tottenham	Lazio	£5.5m
1995	A. Cole	Newcastle	Man. Utd	£7m
1995	D. Bergkamp	Internazionale	Arsenal	£7.5m
1995	S. Collymore	Nottm Forest	Liverpool	£8.5m
1996	A. Shearer	Blackburn	Newcastle	£15m
1999	N. Anelka	Arsenal	Real Madrid	£22.5m
2001	J. Veron	Lazio	Man. Utd	£28.1m
2002	R. Ferdinand	Leeds	Man. Utd	£29.1m

WORLD TRANSFER RECORDS SINCE 1952

Year	Player	From	To	Price
1952	H. Jeppson	Atalanta	Napoli	£52,000
1954	J. Schiaffino	Penarol	Milan	£72,000
1957	E. Sivori	River Plate	Juventus	£93,000
1961	L. Suarez	Barcelona	Inter	£142,000
1963	A. Sormani	Mantova	Roma	£250,000
1968	P. Anastasi	Varese	Juventus	£500,000
1973	J. Cruyff	Ajax	Barcelona	£922,000
1975	G. Savoidi	Bologna	Napoli	£1.2m
1978	P. Rossi	Juventus	Vicenza	£1.75m
1982	D. Maradona	Boca Juniors	Barcelona	£3m
1984	D. Maradona	Barcelona	Napoli	£5m
1987	R. Gullit	PSV Eindhoven	Milan	£6m
1990	R. Baggio	Fiorentina	Juventus	£8m
1992	J.P. Papin	Marseilles	Milan	£10m
1992	G. Vialli	Sampdoria	Juventus	£12m
1992	G. Lentini	Torino	Milan	£13m
1996	A. Shearer	Blackburn	Newcastle	£15m
1997	Ronaldo	Barcelona	Internazionale	£18m

1998	Denilson	Sao Paolo	Real Betis	£22m
1999	C. Vieri	Lazio	Internazionale	£32m
2000	H. Crespo	Parma	Lazio	£35.5m
2000	L. Figo	Barcelona	Real Madrid	£37m
2001	Z. Zidane	Juventus	Real Madrid	£45.62m

World's best-paid footballers: 2003

Again we have a world leader – step forward Becks, but take care, don't trip, don't fall over your wallet, don't mess up your barnet. In 2003 *France Football* calculated that he had made £10 million that year – half from actually playing football, the other half from commercial deals, such as with Vodophone and Marks & Spencer. Actual amounts earned are, of course, estimates, as clubs try never to reveal salaries, but the chances are they have gone up by now – probably by 20 per cent for the top three earners, all of whom, at the time of writing, play for Real Madrid.

TOP 20 EARNERS

1	David Beckham (Real Madrid)	£10.5 million
2	Zinedine Zidane (Real Madrid)	£9.8 million
3	Ronaldo (Real Madrid)	£8.2 million
4	Rio Ferdinand (Manchester United)	£6.75 million
5	Alessandro Del Piero (Juventus)	£6.7 million
6	Hidetoshi Nakata (Parma)	£6.6 million
7	Raul (Real Madrid)	£6.55 million
8	Christian Vieri (Inter Milan)	£6.5 million
9	Michael Owen (Liverpool)	£6.2 million
10	Roy Keane (Manchester United)	£6.05 million
11	Luis Figo (Real Madrid)	£6 million
12	Gabriel Batistuta (Inter Milan)	£6 million
13	Sol Campbell (Arsenal)	£5.7 million
14	Oliver Kahn (Bayern Munich)	£5.4 million
15	Alvaro Recoba (Inter Milan)	£5.35 million
16	Francesco Totti (AS Roma)	£5.1 million

17	Rivaldo (AC Milan)	£5.05 million
18	Thierry Henry (Arsenal)	£4.3 million
19	Fabio Cannavaro (Inter Milan)	£4.2 million
20	Paolo Maldini (AC Milan)	£4.1 million

Source: France Football

Football chants

Part of the fun of going to football is singing songs, belting out chants. If your team happens to have been Spurs in recent years, it's been about the only fun. Football chants are an interesting social phenomenon, part of the dynamics of crowd emotion and reaction. How did each one start, who makes them up, who decides the words, are they ever written down, at which point does the crowd decide to sing them? Ah, all these mysteries.

Most of them are obscene or abusive and therefore unsuitable for a wholesome family book. Many of the more decent, nay, poetic ones, refer to players who are now at different clubs, but the tunes linger on.

Arsenal, when Emmanuel Petit played at Highbury:
He's blond, he's quick,
his name's a porno flick,
Emmanuel, Emmanuel.
He's quick, he's blond,
he's won the Coupe du Monde.

Home sides to **Liverpool** fans, to the tune of *You'll Never Walk Alone:*
Sign on, sign on,
with a pen, in your hand,
cos you'll never get a job,
never get a job.

Liverpool, sung to West Ham fans to the tune of *La donna e mobile:*
You've got Di Canio,
we've nicked your stereo.

Coventry City, to the tune of *In our Liverpool Home:*
In our Coventry homes,
In our Coventry homes,
We speak with an accent
exceedingly rare,
You want a cathedral,
we've got one to spare.
In our Coventry homes.

Exeter City, to the tune of
We'll Meet Again:
  We'll score again,
  Don't know where, don't know
    when,
  But I know we'll score again
  Some sunny day.

Wimbledon, to the tune of
The Wombling Song:
  We won't win the league
    and we won't win the cup.
  We're not going down
    and we're not going up.
  We're not very good,
    in fact we're bad.
  We are the Wombles, we're mad.

Liverpool, praising Stephen
Gerard, to the tune of the Beatles'
Let it Be:
  Spreading balls of wisdom, Stevie G.

Scotland, to the tune of
The Hokey Cokey:
  You put your left hand in,
  You take your left hand out,
  You put your left hand in
    and you shake it all about,
  You do the hokey cokey
    and you turn around
  That's what it's all about.
  Oh, Diego Maradona
  Oh, Diego Maradona
  Oh, Diego Maradona
  He put the English out, out, out.

Footballers and food

Before the FA Cup Final of 1883 between amateurs Old Etonians and professionals Blackburn Olympic, Olympic went to a health hydro near Blackpool for a week's preparation. Olympic were an early Northern, working-class club, unlike the upper-class Etonians, but they did not stint themselves when tucking in. During the week, this was their basic diet:

Pre-breakfast: Glass of port wine at 6am, followed by two raw eggs and a walk along the sands
Breakfast: Porridge and haddock
Lunch: Leg of mutton
Tea: Porridge and a pint of milk
Supper: A dozen oysters each

It seemed to work: Blackburn Olympic beat Old Etonians 2–1, becoming the first non-public school team to win the FA Cup.

The Twelve Days of Christmas

The rules of society: 1860

Food requirements, Victorian era

Factory rules

Management of the infant

Mourning clothes

Victorian underclothes

Advice for a good waaf

HISTORY

The Twelve Days of Christmas

Catholics in England during the period 1558–1839 were prohibited by law from any practice of their faith, public or otherwise. According to a popular urban myth, *The Twelve Days of Christmas* was written as a Catechism Song to help young Catholics memorise the tenets of their faith and avoid being caught with anything in writing.

The **True Love** referred to God himself, the *Me* to every baptised person.

The **Partridge in a Pear Tree** is Jesus Christ the Son of God. In the song, Christ is symbolically presented as a mother partridge, which feigns injury to decoy predators from her helpless nestlings, an expression of Christ's sadness over the fate of Jerusalem.

The **Two Turtle Doves** are the Old and the New Testaments.

The **Three French Hens** are Faith, Hope and Charity, the theological virtues.

The **Four Calling Birds** are the four Gospels and/or the four Evangelists.

The **Five Golden Rings** are the first five books of the Old Testament, which give the history of 'man's' fall from grace.

Six Geese a'Laying are the six days of Creation.

Seven Swans a'Swimming are the seven gifts of the Holy Spirit, the seven sacraments.

Eight Maids a'Milking are the eight beatitudes.

Nine Ladies Dancing are the nine fruits of the Holy Spirit.

Ten Lords a'Leaping are the Ten Commandments.

Eleven Pipers Piping are the eleven faithful apostles.

Twelve Drummers Drumming are the twelve points of doctrine of the Apostles' Creed.

Source: Cumbrian church newsletter

The rules of society, 1860

Social intercourse in the Victorian era was fraught with unspoken rules, especially in terms of visiting. A domestic manual recommended the following:

> 'Those who mix in society are in the habit of reminding one another of their existence, either by personally calling on each other during certain hours, or by merely leaving their cards at the door.'

The visits were made chiefly by ladies and idle men, usually between the hours of 1 and 5 (or 12 and 4 in the country). A call was to last between 15 and 20 minutes and was made at least twice a year and on the following occasions:

1 After the birth of a baby – either in person or by sending a servant.
2 On the marriage of a daughter – usually the day after the wedding.
3 After a death – no calls were made until the lady of the house had sent round her cards 'to return thanks for the inquiries' made during the time of mourning.
4 Prior to a long absence from home – ladies then called on their friends.

Further advice

When the lady making a call is married to a gentleman too busy to make the call with her, it is sufficient if she leaves his card for the master of the house.

In leaving cards for a married couple, a lady usually leaves one card and a gentleman two.

Formal calls on particular occasions should be returned within a few days, 'failing which an apology is due'.

Refreshments don't have to be offered to callers in town, but should in country districts when the caller has come a considerable distance.

Food requirements, Victorian era

Meat and potatoes, along with a pint of malt liquor a day, were regarded as the most important part of a good diet for Victorian men.

'Average daily amount of the best kind of food required by an adult male'

Meat	¾ lb
Bread	¾lb
Potatoes	1½lb
(or green vegetables)	
Cheese	2oz
Butter	1oz
Milk	2oz
Sugar	1oz
Tea	½oz
Coffee	1oz
Malt liquor	1 pint

'Cheap food, sufficient to support an adult in good health'

Bread	1lb
Potatoes	2lb
Peas or beans	4oz
Dripping or lard	4oz
Cabbage or greens	1lb
Cheese	3oz

'Various Kinds of Cheap Food suitable to the Poor Man'

Bullock's, pig's, calf's or sheep's liver, melt or kidney	Sheep's trotters
Pig's blood for black puddings	Sheep's head and pluck
	Cheap fish
Inferior pieces of beef	Peas and beans
	Mushrooms

Factory rules

Factory conditions were notoriously hard in Victorian England, and workers constantly ran the risk of being fined. Here's a list of rules that had to be obeyed in a Lancashire cotton mill in 1851:

Rules to be observed by the hands employed in this mill
Any person coming too late shall be fined as follows:
for 5 minutes 2d, 10 minutes 4d, and 15 minutes 6d

For waste on the floor 2d

For any oil wasted or spilled on the floor 2d each offence, besides paying for the value of the oil

Any person found leaving their work and found talking with any other of the workpeople shall be fined 2d for each offence

For every oath or insolent language, 3d for the first offence, and, if repeated, they shall be dismissed

All persons in our employ shall serve four weeks notice before leaving their employ; but L. Whitaker and Sons shall and will turn any person off without notice being given

The Masters would recommend that all their workpeople wash themselves every morning, but they shall wash themselves at least twice every week, Monday morning and Thursday morning: and any found not washed will be fined 3d for each offence

Any person willfully damaging this notice will be dismissed

Source: Victorian life and transport, *Richard Dunning, 1981*

Management of the infant

If you thought detailed lists of everything required for newborn babies was a 21st-century trend, then consider the advice contained in an 1857 *Manual of Domestic Economy:*

Articles required for infant management
1. A low chair, with or without rockers
2. A footstool
3. Two thick flannel aprons
4. One large washing basin
5. One soap-dish and soap (best yellow or white curd)
6. One small enamel saucepan
7. One semi-porcelain pipkin and lamp
8. One pap-boat (silver or crockery)
9. One feeding-bottle, with two or three nipples
10. One small jug
11. One tea-spoon and one dessert-spoon
12. One small pot de chamber, with two flannel covers

The above list was intended for a baby's first month. The semi-porcelain pipkin and lamp was 'a most useful modern invention' used to warm water and food. The pap-boat was used to 'force' the baby to take disagreeables, either in the shape of food or medicine. The nipples on the feeding bottle should be India-rubber, preferred to the traditional hollowed-out cow teat or sewn-up wash-leather – both of which were liable to become semi-putrid.

Mourning clothes

When it came to mourning the passing of a loved one, Victorian women had to follow a strict protocol, whereas men could normally get away with a hatband and a black suit.

Wife for husband
1 year, 1 month: bombazine covered with crepe; widow's cap,
    lawn cuffs, collars

Daughter for parent
6 months: black with black or white crepe (for young girls); no
    linen cuffs and collars; no jewellery for first 2 months

Mother for child
6 months: black with crepe; no linen cuffs and collars; no
    jewellery for first 2 months

Mother for infant
3 months, often with no crepe

Wife for husband's parents
18 months in black bombazine with crepe

Victorian underclothes

Victorian women were 'incredibly modest', recalls Gwen Raverat, one
chronicler of the times. 'You could see a friend in her petticoat, but
nothing below that was considered decent.' While 'decent' women
didn't take much trouble with their underclothes, these garments could
be complicated, favouring the layered method of dress. In her 1952
memoir, Raverat describes sharing a room one night with a young lady
who was wearing the following underclothes:

1 Thick, long-legged, long-sleeved woollen combinations
2 Over them, white cotton combinations, with plenty of
    buttons and frills
3 Very serious, bony, gray stays, with suspenders
4 Black woollen stockings
5 White cotton drawers, with buttons and frills

6 White cotton 'petticoat-bodice', with embroidery, buttons
and frills
7 Rather short, white flannel petticoat
8 Long alpaca petticoat, with a flounce round the bottom
9 Pink flannel blouse

Source: Gwen Raverat (1885–1957) wood engraver and illustrator,
granddaughter of Charles Darwin, quoted in The Victorian House,
Judith Flanders, 2003

Advice for a good WAAF

In 1940 Deirdre Byer was already in the Women's Air Force, helping to
win the war. Her younger sister, Elizabeth, was just about to join up –
so Deirdre wrote her a list, telling her what she should bring and what
she might expect:

2 prs pyjamas

1 dressing gown

1 pr slippers

Toilet things in a waterproof bag

Make-up

Natural nail varnish

Large duster

1 small brush (for boots)

1 small brush (cleaning buttons)

1 button stick

1 large tin Silvo

Large tin Cherry Blossom – this will
shortly be rationed

Large supply of paper, ink, envelopes
and stamps if desirous of not giving
up friends (male)

Two black ties – if you can obtain
them without coupons

Some fine hairnets with elastic – to
keep your hair off your collar

Hairbrush, comb, grips

Soap and towel – there is a plain one
of mine in my drawer, but don't you
dare get it swiped

DO'S

Accept all garments given you on kitting-out parade,
even if they don't fit you, even if you don't wear them, as
you will have to produce them on kit inspection.

When cleaning buttons, put button stick through
buttons, apply Silvo heavily and burn with a match. The
Silvo will run off in a thick brown liquid. Apply more
Silvo, allow to dry and brush well. Finish off with the
duster. Do cap badge in similar manner.

DON'TS

Wear your hat on one side.

Wear your stockings inside out.

Never cut a service article of clothing.

Forget to clean buttons and shoes.

Don't take anything of value – it will be swiped.

Don't get downhearted.

There is only one 'don't' I have forgotten. I should have
told you ages ago. Don't join the forces...

PEOPLE'S
FUNNY
WAYS

Strange things sent through the post

The National Return Letter Centre in the UK deals with millions of undeliverable mail each year – of which a quarter are said to be successfully redelivered. Here's a list of some of the stranger things sent through the post.

A live snake

A mummified hand

A putrid salmon

Thousands of Christmas cards without addresses

An old-fashioned wooden leg

Thousands of Valentine's cards without addresses

£25,000 cash in an envelope (accidentally posted, it was supposed to go into the night safe of a big department store via internal mail)

Lots of underwear

Letters addressed to fictional characters – Santa Claus, Peggy Mitchell, Dot Cotton (both *Eastenders* characters)

Letters, without addresses, to famous football players

Source: article in The Guardian

Body decoration

One in five Britons now has a tattoo – with men preferring their arm tattooed and women opting for their back, shoulder or leg. But even more people – 48 per cent according to a survey in the *Observer* – now have a piercing somewhere on their body. Pierced genitals are just as popular as pierced eyebrows.

Most popular places for tattoos	Percentage
Arms	51
Back	30
Shoulders	27
Legs	17
Breasts/chest	10
Bottom	9
Stomach	7
Hands	6
Neck	4
Feet	3
Other	3

Most popular places for piercing	Percentage
Ears	94
Navel	11
Nose	7
Nipples	4
Tongue	4
Eyebrow	3
Genitals	3
Lips	3

Source: Observer survey

Fear of flying

Fear of flying is one of the most common fears there is. People know it's largely irrational, but that doesn't make it any easier to bear. Those who fear flying are also likely to fear heights, are petrified of being driven by another car driver, and are pretty scared of boats. However, they tend not to fear train rides at all.

The following comes from a survey of those who suffer from fear of flying.

Percentage who also suffer from:

Panic attacks	11
Claustrophobia	22
Fear of heights	67
Fear of driving	11
Fear of being driven by some other drivers	89
Fear of being driven by all other drivers	22
Fear of trains	0
Fear of boats	44
Fear of lifts	33
Fear of escalators	11
Fear of fairground rides	78

And here's self-help guru Allen Carr's advice on how to conquer a fear of flying for good.

Follow all the instructions

Keep an open mind

Start off in a happy frame of mind

Think positively

Go for it!

Enjoy it!

Do not try to take your mind off the flight

You are going to take control

Don't try to fly the plane!

Source: The easy way to enjoy flying, *Allen Carr, 2000*

Job applications

The list below contains exerpts from CVs and covering letters…

1   'I have lurnt Word Perfect 6.0 computor and spreadsheet programs.'

2   'Am a perfectionist and rarely if ever forget details.'

3   'Received a plague for Salesperson of the Year.'

4   'Wholly responsible for two (2) failed financial institutions.'

5   'Reason for leaving last job: maturity leave.'

6   'Failed bar exam with relatively high grades.'

7   'It's best for employers that I not work with people.'

8   'Let's meet, so you can 'ooh' and 'aah' over my experience.'

9   'I was working for my mum until she decided to move.'

10 'Marital status: single. Unmarried. Unengaged. Uninvolved. No commitments.'

11 'I have an excellent track record, although I am not a horse.'

12 'I am loyal to my employer at all costs. Please feel free to respond to my resume on my office voicemail.'

13 'My goal is to be a meteorologist. But since I possess no training in meteorology, I suppose I should try stockbroking.'

14 'I procrastinate, especially when the task is unpleasant.'

15 'Personal interests: donating blood. Fourteen gallons so far.'

16 'Instrumental in ruining entire operation for a chain store.'

17 'Note: Please don't misconstrue my 14 jobs as 'job-hopping'. I have never quit a job.'

18 'Marital status: often. Children: various.'

19 'The company made me a scapegoat, just like my three previous employers.'

20 'Finished eighth in my class of ten.'

21 'References: none. I've left a path of destruction behind me.'

Dollar billionaires

London has the highest number of dollar billionaires in the world. The following is a list of dollar billionaires throughout the world in 2004.

London	40
New York	31
Moscow	23
Geneva	20
Los Angeles	18
Hong Kong	16
San Francisco	15
Dallas	14
Tokyo	10
Paris	10
Mexico City	9
Seattle	9
Chicago	7
Boston	6
Palm Beach	6
Singapore	6
Taipei	6
Hamburg	5
Toronto	5
Milan	2

Source: Sunday Times

Excuses for late payment

Anyone who has dealings with companies knows it can take ages to receive payment for services rendered. A survey by the Better Payment Practice Group found that the most common excuse given for late payment was that the company was waiting for the cheque to be signed. More imaginative excuses included the assertion that the cheque book had been buried, along with its deceased owner.

Most common excuses for late payment	Percentage
1 Waiting for the cheque to be signed	23
2 Lost the invoice, send a copy	22
3 Cashflow problems, waiting for debtors to pay us	16
4 Account handler is off sick or is unavailable	15
5 Cheque is in the post	6
6 New computer system being installed or has failed	6
7 Waiting for new cheque book or have run out of cheques	5
8 Invoice in dispute	3
9 We pay on 60/90 days, not 30 days	2
10 You've missed the payment run	2

More bizarre excuses

'The cheque book has been destroyed in the flood.'

'The owner's been buried with his cheque book.'

'The director went for an operation and never returned, as he went off with the nurse.'

'The tide is out and the director is unable to get in to pay cheques.'

'I cannot make payment until the planets are aligned, which is only twice a year.'

'We're in the middle of an armed robbery.'

'Not now, it's the office party.'

Top hobbies

Londoners would rather be at the pub than join a yoga class or engage in charity work, but their favourite leisure activity is eating out. Cooking, gardening and DIY have also become more popular, due to the increase in lifestyle television shows. Less than two per cent of people have given yoga a try, but nine per cent regularly attend bingo sessions.

Top 10 London hobbies
1 Eating out
2 Reading
3 Foreign travel
4 Pub
5 Cookery
6 Gardening
7 Fashion
8 DIY
9 Cinema
10 Gym

Source: report by marketing solutions company CACI

Most common dreams

The average person spends a quarter of each night dreaming – which adds up to about six years of their life. The most vivid dreams happen during a type of sleep called Rapid Eye Movement (REM) when the brain is very active and the eyes move back and forth under the lids.

The ancient Greeks believed that dreams could reveal important things about our health. Recent research has shown that people who say they never dream have the highest mortality rate.

**Top 10 most common dreams in the
1980s, according to *Prediction Magazine***

1 Houses
2 Water
3 Aeroplanes
4 Snakes
5 Doors
6 Eyes
7 A tower
8 A tree
9 Teeth
10 Mountains

Top 10 most common dreams in 2004

Falling is one of today's most common dreams. It can
mean the dreamer fears losing respect, or can indicate
money problems. If you land and wake suddenly then
this is a 'wake-up call' to attend to matters in the physical
world.

Dreaming about a house is another very common dream.
A house usually represents yourself, with rooms
representing different aspects. Doors are opportunities.

Car dreams are also common. The meaning depends on:
Who is driving? Is it a pleasant journey? What is the state
of the car? Cars are a symbol of power, status and vitality.

Animals: wild animals denote fears and even misfortune.
Domestic animals usually mean good fortune.

Celebrities: people don't dream as much about God or
the Devil anymore, instead they dream about meeting or
becoming a famous person. These tend to be happy,
positive dreams suggesting that a goal can finally be
achieved.

Being chased: a dream linked to anxiety, which suggests the dreamer is running away from something. If you escape the chase then your life quest is taking a new road.

Death: although scary, dreaming about someone else's or your own death can actually signify that a rebirth is about to occur in your life.

Flying: this indicates the dreamer is trying to exercise free choice in their life.

Being lost: the meaning is literal – you are lost in your life, adrift.

Being naked in a public place: clothes symbolise your outer expression, being naked can suggest you are letting down the walls that surround you.

People's tastes in reading also affect dreams. The results of a Dream Lab experiment, which surveyed 100,000 people, showed:

Readers of fiction have the most bizarre dreams

People who read romance books are more likely to tell their dreams to other people

There is no relation between reading crime or thriller books and having nightmares

People who sleep for long hours go to a library more often than those whose sleep is short

Sources:
www.webspawner.com
www.saga.co.uk
www.kindredspirit.co.uk

Weird phobias

At least a quarter of people are said to be affected by one kind of phobia or another, often a fear of spiders or heights. Here are some lesser-known fears:

Alektorophobia – fear of chickens
Alliumphobia – fear of garlic
Anthrophobia – fear of flowers
Arachibutyrophobia – fear of peanut butter sticking to the roof of the mouth
Athazagoraphobia – a fear of forgetting things
Automatonophobia – fear of ventriloquists' dummies
Batophobia – fear of being close to high buildings
Bogyphobia – fear of the bogeyman
Chronophobia – fear of time
Cnidophobia – fear of string
Coulrophobia – fear of clowns
Deipnophobia – fear of dinner conversations
Ergasiophobia – a fear of work
Geniophobia – fear of chins
Hellenologophobia – a fear of Greek words and scientific terms
Hippopotomonstrosesquippedaliophobia – fear of long words
Lachanophobia – fear of vegetables
Mageirocophobia – fear of cooking
Metrophobia – fear of poetry
Ostraconophobia – fear of shellfish
Panophobia – fear of everything
Phobophobia – fear of fear
Pogonophobia – a fear of beards
Pteronophobia – fear of being tickled by feathers
Rupophobia – a fear of dirt
Triskaidekaphobia – a fear of the number 13
Xanthophobia – a fear of the colour yellow

Office romance

People who work in marketing or advertising have a pretty good chance of an affair with a work colleague – unlike architects who are more likely to keep business and pleasure separate.

A study by Tiscali.co.uk, the Internet service provider, found that most people began their relationship by flirting in the corridor at work.

Percentage of people who have had a romantic involvement with a work colleague

Marketing/Advertising	93
Pharmaceuticals	85
Telecoms	73
Financial Services	69
Sales	62
Accountancy	59
Law	57
IT	54
Broadcasting	52
Education	51
Retail	50
Banking	50
Design	49
Property	49
Media/TV	48
Social Services	48
Leisure	48
Hotels	47
Publishing	47
Tourism/Travel Agents	46
Events	46
Insurance	46
Office Admin	46
Recruitment	45
Civil Service	44
Charity	43

Internet/New Media	41
Research	34
Architecture	33

Lonely Hearts ads

How many people tell the truth when they are searching, or advertising, for a soulmate? The following list is a guide to what might be behind people's descriptions of themselves:

Women seeking Men

40-ish = 48
Adventurous = Has had more partners than you ever will
Affectionate = Possessive
Artist = Unreliable
Commitment-minded = Pick out curtains, now
Communication important = Just try to get a word in edgeways
Consistent = Fifteenth ad placed this year
Fun = Annoying
Light drinker = Lush

Men seeking Women

40-ish = 52 and looking for 25 year old
Artist = Delicate ego badly in need of massage
Educated = Will aways treat you like an idiot
Fun = Good with a remote and a six pack
Honest = Pathological liar
Like romantic walks on the beach = Reads *Cosmo* and thinks this is what you want to hear
Physically fit = Spends a lot of time in front of mirrors admiring himself
Sensitive = Needy

Source: The House of Lists (web site)

Most popular names

After six years, the name Chloe has finally been knocked off the top spot by Emily, now the UK's most popular girl's name – and the most popular name in the USA since 1996.

In terms of boys' names, Jack has been the most popular for nine years – it remains popular in Northern Ireland, Scotland, the Republic of Ireland and New Zealand, but far less so in the USA and Australia.

The rise in the popularity of Alfie is attributed to a character in UK TV soap *EastEnders*, while the rise in the girl's name Chardonnay is attributed to a character in the UK TV drama *Footballer's Wives*.

The most popular baby names in the UK, 2003

Male	Female
Jack	Emily
Joshua	Ellie
Thomas	Chloe
James	Jessica
Daniel	Sophie

The list above comes from the National Statistics Office, but consider the top names of 2003 according to the website BabyNames.com:

Male	Female
Aidan	Madison
Jaden	Emma
Caden	Abigail
Ethan	Riley
Caleb	Chloe

Historically, John is one of the longest-running favourite boys' names dating back to 1800, while Sarah has been one of the top girls' names for almost 200 years.

Top names in the UK, 1800

Male	Female	Male	Female
		In the USA	
Male	*Female*	*Male*	*Female*
William	Mary	John	Mary
John	Ann	William	Anna
Thomas	Elizabeth	Charles	Elizabeth
James	Sarah	George	Margaret
George	Jane	James	Minnie

Top names in the UK, 1900

Male	Female	Male	Female
		In the USA	
Male	*Female*	*Male*	*Female*
William	Florence	John	Mary
John	Mary	William	Helen
George	Alice	James	Anna
Thomas	Annie	George	Margaret
Charles	Elsie	Charles	Ruth

Top names in the UK, 1950

Male	Female	Male	Female
		In the USA	
Male	*Female*	*Male*	*Female*
David	Susan	John	Linda
John	Linda	James	Mary
Peter	Margaret	Robert	Patricia
Michael	Carol	William	Barbara
Alan	Jennifer	Michael	Susan

Top names in the UK, 1975

Male	Female
Stephen	Sarah
Mark	Nicole
Paul	Emma
Andrew	Joanne
David	Helen

In the USA

Male	Female
Michael	Jennifer
Christopher	Amy
Jason	Michelle
David	Heather
James	Angela
Robert (tie)	

Top names in the UK, 1988

Male	Female
Daniel	Rebecca
Christopher	Sarah
Michael	Emma
James	Laura
Matthew	Rachel

In the USA

Male	Female
Michael	Ashley
Christopher	Jessica
Matthew	Amanda
Joshua	Jennifer
David	Brittany

Sources:
For top UK names: www.worldzone.net (with credit to
The Guinness Book of Names*) and National Statistics Office.*
For top USA names: Social Security Administration, names taken from a survey of Social Security Card applications (note: different spellings of similar names are considered separate names in these tables)

Wish list

Water activities top the list when it comes to the things people want to do before they die. Swimming with dolphins is the number one dream, according to a BBC poll of 20,000 people. High on the list are physical challenges in far-off places, and getting in touch with animals. Number three on the list will remain the ultimate in wishful thinking as Concorde has now retired.

Swim with dolphins

Scuba dive on the Great Barrier Reef

Fly Concorde to New York

Go whale-watching

Dive with sharks

Skydive

Fly in a hot air balloon

Fly in a fighter jet

Go on safari

See the Northern Lights

PETS

Strange animal behaviour

'It's raining cats and dogs' might just be an expression, but there have been instances when it has rained fish and frogs. The probable reason is when mini-tornadoes scoop up water and small fish and then dump them on land. In 1976 Olympic yachts were even pelted by live maggots.

Falling fish

Aberdare, Mid Glamorgan	1841, 1859
Singapore	1861
Worcester	1881
Bournemouth	1948
Sunderland, Tyne and Wear	1918
London	1984
Ipswich, Australia	1989
Great Yarmouth, Norfolk	2000

Falling frogs

Bedford	1979
Llanddewi, Wales	1996
Croydon, Surrey	1998, 2000

Falling turtle

Mississippi, USA	1930

Falling corn

Evans, Colorado, USA	1982–86

Falling alligators

South Carolina, USA	1877

Sources: www.uktouristinfo.com, http://news.bbc.co.uk,
http://paranormal.miningco.com

Top cat names

The naming of cats is a difficult matter. A cat needs a name, that's particular, a name that's unusual, and more dignified, else how can he keep up his tail perpendicular? T.S. ELLIOT

More Britons now own cats than they do dogs. Many family moggies are named after singing stars like Elvis and Britney. But some of the traditional favourites hark back to Latin – like the ever-popular Felix, which means 'fortunate'.

Top 5 cat names
1 Sooty
2 Tigger
3 Lucy
4 Smokey
5 Charlie

Source: www.petplanet.co.uk

Cat facts
40% of people say cats are their favourite pets (compared with 7% preferring dogs)

57% of people like cats because they are affectionate

49% like cats for their independence

46% like them because they are clean

27% say they like not having to exercise cats

Cats are most popular with the 35–44 age group (nearly a third of people in this age group own a cat)

Two-thirds of cat owners say curling up with their cat is the best way to deal with stress (preferable to speaking to a friend or going for a drink)

50% of people – both women and men – would rather wake up with their cat than their partner

98% of women would rather date someone who likes cats

Source: survey conducted by the Cats Protection League

Top dog names

Almost a quarter of UK households own a dog as a pet, spending on average £7 a week on food, bedding and toys. Twenty-five years ago the most popular names for male dogs came from drinks, or famous dogs on TV or in film. Today many people give their dog a human name – with many called after footballing heroes like Becks and Zola.

Top 5 dog names, 1980

Male	*Female*
1 Shep	1 Sheba
2 Brandy	2 Sally
3 Whisky	3 Rosie
4 Patch	4 Mandy
5 Butch	5 Tessa

Source: NCDL

Top 5 dog names, 2004

Male	*Female*
1 Sam	1 Trixie
2 Spot	2 Polly
3 Pip	3 Jessie
4 Duke	4 Lucy
5 Piper	5 Bonnie

Source: PetPlanet

Top 5 dog names, USA, 2004

Male	*Female*
1 Max	1 Maggie
2 Jake	2 Bear
3 Buddy	3 Molly
4 Bear	4 Shadow
5 Bailey	5 Lucy

Source: bowwow.com

Most popular dog breeds

Traditional British dogs such as terriers, corgis and sheepdogs have lost popularity in recent years, to be replaced by the latest foreign breed – and sometime fashion accessory – the Shih-tzu, which originates in Tibet.

Dog breeds come and go, with the Dalmatian popular in the late 19th century, the poodle in the 1950s, the long-haired Afghan hound in the 1970s and the 'macho' pit bulls in the 1990s. Some people fear British breeds could die out altogether, with the number of registered Yorkshire terriers, for example, dropping by almost 70 per cent. The reason could be a change in lifestyle, with a decline in rural life, or a trend among celebrities to favour more exotic breeds. The Shih-tzu reportedly doesn't really need taking out for walks.

Most popular foreign breeds in the UK

Labrador retriever (Canada)	35,996
German shepherd	14,177
Boxer (German)	8,916
Rottweiler	5,802
Shih-tzu (Tibet)	3,113

Least popular British breeds

Glen of Imaal terrier	48
Otterhound	54
English toy terrier	56
Welsh Corgi	56
Sealyham terrier	58

Source: the Independent

Endangered species

Almost 1,000 species are now officially endangered in the USA –
covering 985 animals and 597 plants.

Mammals	65
Birds	78
Reptiles	14
Amphibians	12
Fishes	71
Clams	62
Snails	21
Insects	35
Arachnids	12
Crustaceans	18
Flowering plants	569
Conifers, Cycads	2
Ferns, Allies	24
Lichens	2

Source: Threatened and Endangered Species System, US Government

African animal proverbs

A dog knows the places he is thrown food
　　Luyia, Western Kenya

A donkey knows no gratitude
　　Swahili

A hyena cannot smell its own stench
  Kalenjin, Kenya

Dogs do not actually prefer bones to meat, it is just that no-one ever gives them meat
  Akan, West Africa

He flees from the roaring lion to the crouching lion
  Sechuana

That man's a fool whose sheep flees twice
  Oji

The elephant never gets tired of carrying its tusks
  Vai, Liberia

The frog does not run in the daytime for nothing
  Igbo, Nigeria

Chinese animal proverbs

A bird in your hand is worth more than 100 in the forest

How can you expect to find ivory in a dog's mouth?

Vicious as a tigress can be, she never eats her own cubs

You can't catch a cub without going into the tiger's den

You think you lost your horse? Who knows he may bring a whole herd back to you someday

Source: www.famous-proverbs.com

World's top tourist destinations

World's costliest cities

Top Paris attractions

Most fascinating urinals

Odd town names

Dirtiest places in the UK

The UK's dirtiest roads

Most polluted parks in the USA

Stress in the cities, USA

Burglary hot spots in the UK

Survey of USA cities

Top honeymoon destinations

Top 10 theme parks in the USA

Global weather extremes

Most destructive earthquakes

Most visited attractions in the UK

Top 5 lawns in the USA

PLACES

World's top tourist destinations

Destination	Visitors, in millions
France	76.5
Spain	49.5
United States	45.5
Italy	39.0
China	33.2
UK	23.4
Russia	21.1
Mexico	19.8
Canada	19.7
Austria	18.2

Source: World Tourism Organisation, 2001 figures

World's costliest cities

Osaka/Kobe
Tokyo
Hong Kong
Libreville
Oslo
London
New York
Zurich
Singapore
Taipei
Tel Aviv

Source: Economist Intelligence Unit

Top Paris attractions

Here's a list of the attractions most visited in Paris, France. Museums remain the most popular, with 4 in the Top 6 for 2002:

Destination	Visitors, in millions
Eiffel Tower	6.2
Louvre Museum	5.7
Pompidou Centre	5.5
Cité des Sciences et de l'Industrie	2.5
Musée d'Orsay	2.1
Arc de Triomphe	1.4

Source: gofrance.about.com, Paris Office of Tourism Statistics

Most fascinating urinals

Do you have a favourite urinal? Perhaps you've even taken a photo of it. If so, then you can vote for the world's most fascinating urinals, and submit your illustration, at the website urinal.net. It ranks the following urinals as its Top 10:

1. Amundsen-Scott South Pole Station — South Pole, Antarctica
2. Hong Kong Sheraton Hotel and Towers — Hong Kong
3. Public Rest Rooms of Rothesay — Rothesay, Isle of Bute, UK
4. The Millennium Dome — London, England
5. Women's Urinal at Dairy Queen — Port Charlotte, FL, USA
6. The Felix — Hong Kong
7. International Space Station — In Space
8. John Michael Kohler Arts Center — Sheboygan, WI, USA
9. Madonna Inn — San Luis Obispo, CA, USA
10. TV Hill — Kabul, Afghanistan

Odd town names

A town named Cool may not be that surprising in a state like California, but how about Intercourse in Pennsylvania? In England, town names often suggest sleepiness, like Great Snoring in Norfolk and Land of Nod in Devon.

Here's a selection of some of the odder town names in the UK, USA and Canada.

UK

Brown Willey, Cornwall
California, Norfolk
Crackpot, North Yorks
Effingham, Surrey
Egypt, Hampshire
Eye, Suffolk
Foul Mile, East Sussex
Giggleswick, North Yorkshire
Great Snoring, Norfolk
Ham and Sandwich, Kent
Land of Nod, Devon
Little Snoring, Norfolk
Mousehole, Cornwall
Nasty, Hertfordshire
New Invention, Wales
North Piddle, Worcestershire
Pity Me, Co. Durham
Shop, Cornwall
Steeple Bumpstead,
   Cambridgeshire
Thong, Kent
Twatt, Orkney and Shetland
Wetwang With Fimber, Yorkshire
Windy Yet, Strathclyde, Scotland

USA

Normal, Alabama
Slapout, Alabama
Chicken, Alaska
Dead Horse, Alaska
Santa Claus, Arizona, Georgia
   and Indiana
Why, Arizona
Toad Suck, Arkansas
Cool, California
Likely, California
Climax, Colorado, Georgia,
   Michigan and Pennsylvania
Hygiene, Colorado
No Name, Colorado
Nowhere, Colorado
Paradox, Colorado
Cook's Hammock, Florida
Frostproof, Florida
Niceville, Florida
Between, Georgia
Experiment, Georgia
Hopeulikeit, Georgia
Po Biddy Crossroads, Georgia
Beer Bottle Crossing, Idaho

USA (continued)

Assumption, Illinois
Normal, Illinois
Bacon, Indiana
Loafers Station, Indiana
Surprise, Indiana
Smileyberg, Kansas
Big Bone Lick State Park,
    Kentucky
Cadillac, Kentucky
Chevrolet, Kentucky
Lovely, Kentucky
Ono, Kentucky
Ordinary, Kentucky
Waterproof, Louisiana
Accident, Maryland
Boring, Maryland
Hell, Michigan
Hells Creek Bottom, Mississippi
Hot Coffee, Mississippi
Money, Mississippi
Peculiar, Missouri

Tightwad, Missouri
Truth Or Consequences, New
    Mexico
Okay, Oklahoma
Boring, Oregon
Intercourse, Pennsylvania
Difficult, Tennessee
Cut and Shoot, Texas
Petty, Texas
Telephone, Texas
Bread Loaf, Vermont
Odd, West Virginia
Sod, West Virginia

Canada

Come-by–Chance,
    Newfoundland
St. Louis de Ha! Ha!, Quebec
Economy, Nova Scotia
Lower Economy, Nova Scotia
Upper Economy, Nova Scotia

Source: http://s88932719.onlinehome.us/townname.htm

Dirtiest places in the UK

Ninety per cent of the UK is now affected by some sort of pollution – whether air, noise or light. Light pollution means that more than half of us will never see the Milky Way from our homes, thanks to the increase in street lamps, sport floodlights and private security lights. The least polluted region in England is Northumberland, where there are three times as many sheep as people.

Top 10 dirty places in the UK

1 London	6 Cardiff
2 Reading	7 Birmingham
3 Glasgow	8 Southampton
4 Bradford	9 Manchester
5 Belfast	10 Brighton

Source: BBC survey

Britain's dirtiest roads

According to government scientists, 761 roads in the UK will still be breaking air pollution standards in 2005, with forecast levels of nitrogen dioxide exceeding government targets. London has 595 of the most polluted roads. Birmingham comes second, followed by Bristol and Doncaster.

Top 4 polluted roads

Park Lane in London's West End

The North Circular Road in Hendon, London

Wellington Road, Leeds

Grosvenor Place, near Buckingham Palace, London

Source: Friends of the Earth, Country Life

Most polluted parks in the USA

Many of the national parks in the United States have the dirtiest air in the country, even worse than heavily polluted cities like Los Angeles. The air pollution comes from burning fossil fuels – coal, oil and gas. The following parks are ranked as the worst:

1 Great Smoky Mountains National Park, Tennessee and North Carolina – ozone pollution rivals that of Los Angeles.
2 Shenandoah National Park, Virginia – views from Skyline Drive and the Appalachian Trail shrink to 1 mile on some summer days thanks to fine-particle pollution.
3 Mammoth Cave National Park, Kentucky – ridge top views are among the haziest in the country and, on average, rainfall in the park is ten times more acidic than natural conditions.
4 Sequoia and Kings Canyon National Parks, California.
5 Acadia National Park, Maine.

Stress in the cities, USA

Tacoma, Washington, is America's most stressful city, in terms of unemployment, divorce, commuting time, violent and property crime, suicide, alcohol consumption, self-reported 'poor mental health' and number of cloudy days. Sperling's, an American firm that prides itself on helping people to find the best place to live, has ranked 100 largest metro areas according to stress levels:

Most stressful cities
Tacoma, WA – high divorce and unemployment rate, lots of cloudy days, but low violent-crime rate.
Miami, FL – highest violent-crime rate, but plenty of 'positive mental attitude' among residents.
New Orleans – high levels of violent crime and unemployment.

Las Vegas, NV – highest suicide and divorce rate, but the
greatest number of sunny days.
New York, NY – the longest commute for workers, but
low suicide and divorce rates.

Least stressful cities
Albany-Schenectady-Troy, NY, and Harrisburg-Lebanon-
Carlisle, PA – both areas score well, despite dreary
winters.
Orange Country, CA – very low suicide rate.
Nassau-Suffolk, NY – lowest violent- and property-crime
rates.
Minneapolis-St Paul, MN – low unemployment and
violent crime, but many cloudy days.

Burglary hot spots in the UK

West Yorkshire has the highest levels of burglary in England and Wales,
according to Home Office statistics. The overall average is 202
burglaries a year per 10,000 properties, but in West Yorkshire it's 426.
The high figures have been blamed on easy motorway access into the
area, officers redeployed to deal with other crimes and an understaffed
police force (the fourth largest in England and Wales).

On the other end of the scale, Dyfed-powys has just 32 break-ins per
10,000 properties. This is attributed to neighbourhood policing, a
strong sense of community and plenty of neighbourhood watch
schemes.

But this may not be the true picture, as the Home Office estimates
only 65 per cent of domestic burglaries are reported to the police and
of these just 71 per cent are actually recorded.

Burglary highs and lows

Number of burglaries per 10,000 households, a selection of Home
Office statistics for the year ending April 2003:

Avon and Somerset	234
Beds	168
Cambridge	189
Cheshire	158
City of London	106
Cleveland	328
Devon and Cornwall	107
Dorset	98
Dyfed-powys	32
Greater Manchester	408
Humberside	334
Metropolitan	240
North Wales	116
Notts	382
Suffolk	81
West Midlands	261
West Yorkshire	426

Survey of USA cities

Amherst, NY, is the safest city in the United States, while Detroit, MI, is
the most dangerous, according to publishing and research company
Morgan Quitno Press, which surveyed 322 cities.

Safest	Most dangerous
Amherst, NY	Detroit, MI
Mission Viejo, CA	Atlanta, GA
Brick Township, NJ	St Louis, MO
Newton, MA	Flint, MI
Simi Valley, CA	Camden, NJ

Top honeymoon destinations

According to an annual survey carried out by the American magazine *Modern Bride*, the most popular honeymoon destination is Aruba in the Caribbean, with England coming in at 17th place.

Top 20

1	Aruba	11	US Virgin Islands
2	Bermuda	12	France
3	Florida	13	British Virgin Islands
4	Hawaii	14	Fiji
5	Italy	15	Bahamas
6	Jamaica	16	Dominican Republic
7	Las Vegas	17	England
8	Mexico	18	Greece
9	St Lucia	19	Bali
10	Tahiti	20	Africa

Top 10 theme parks in the USA

In 2002 Florida led the pack when it came to American theme parks, with 7 of the nation's Top 10 located in this sunshine state.

	Destination	Visitors, in millions
1	The Magic Kingdom, Walt Disney World, Lake Buena Vista, FL	14.0
2	Disneyland, Anaheim, CA	12.7
3	Epcot, Walt Disney World, Lake Buena Vista, FL	8.3
4	Disney-MGM Studios, Walt Disney World, Lake Buena Vista, FL	8.0
5	Disney's Animal Kingdom, Walt Disney World, Lake Buena Vista, FL	7.3

6	Universal Studios at Universal Orlando, FL	6.9
7	Islands of Adventure at Universal Orlando, FL	6.1
8	Universal Studios Hollywood, Universal City, CA	5.2
9	SeaWorld Florida, Orlando, FL	5.0
10	Disney's California Adventure, Anaheim, CA	4.7

Source: Amusement Business Magazine

Global weather extremes

In 1922 Libya recorded the highest measured temperature ever, with 136°F. On the other end of the scale, Vostok in Antarctica had the lowest measured temperature of -129°F, in 1983.

Highest temperatures

Place	*°F*	*Date*
1 El Azizia, Libya	136	13 September 1922
2 Death Valley, California	134	10 July, 1913
3 Tirat Tsvi, Israel, SW Asia	129	21 June, 1942
4 Cloncurry, Queensland	128	16 January, 1889
5 Seville, Spain	122	4 August, 1881

Lowest temperatures

1 Vostok, Antarctica	-129	21 July, 1983
2 Oimekon, Russia	-90	6 February, 1933
3 Verkhoyansk, Russia	-90	7 February, 1892
4 Northice, Greenland	-87	9 January, 1954
5 Snag, Yukon, Canada	-81.4	3 February, 1947

Source: National Climatic Data Center

Most destructive earthquakes

The most destructive earthquake ever recorded happened in China in 1556, although some of the worst quakes date back to before 1000AD.

Date	Location	Deaths
23 January, 1556	China, Shansi	830,000
27 July, 1976	China, Tangshan	255,000
	(= official; estimated: 655,000)	
9 August, 1138	Syria, Aleppo	230,000
22 May, 1927	China, near Xining	200,000
22 December, 856	Iran, Damghan	200,000
16 December, 1920	China, Gansu	200,000
23 March, 893	Iran, Ardabil	150,000
1 September, 1923	Japan, Kwanto	143,000
5 October, 1948	USSR	110,000
28 December, 1908	Italy, Messina	up to 100,000

Source: US Department of the Interior, US Geological Survey

Most visited attractions in the UK

Or, at least, places where heads can be counted and numbers compared – not, of course, that like is being compared with like. There have been some striking differences over the last 25 years, as the lists show. As now, back in 1979 places like the British Museum and the Science Museum did not charge for entrance. Since 1979 we have also seen the arrival of new commercially run tourist attractions, such as the Eden Project in Cornwall.

Top 10 attractions, 1979	Attendance
1 Tower of London	2,749,000
2 State Apartments, Windsor Castle	820,000
3 Roman Baths & Pump Room, Bath	709,000

4	Stonehenge, Wiltshire	674,000
5	Shakespeare's birthplace, Stratford-upon-Avon	576,000
6	Beaulieu, Hampshire	566,000
7	Hampton Court, London	556,000
8	St George's Chapel, Windsor	545,000
9	Warwick Castle	467,000
10	Salisbury Cathedral, Wiltshire	450,000

Top 10 attractions, 2003		*Attendance*
1	Blackpool Pleasure Beach	5,737,000
2	British Museum	4,584,000
3	Tate Modern	3,895,746
4	Natural History Museum	2,976,738
5	Science Museum	2,886,859
6	Victoria & Albert Museum	2,257,325
7	Tower of London	1,972,263
8	Eden Project	1,404,737
9	Legoland Windsor	1,321,128
10	National Maritime Museum	1,305,150

Top 5 lawns in the USA

New York's Central Park has the nation's best lawn, combining a well-kept turf with the impressive view of the city's skyline. The following is a list of the Top 5 lawns of 2003, according to small engine manufacturer Briggs & Stratton, which produces outdoor power equipment such as lawnmowers:

1 Central Park's Great Lawn – New York, New York
2 Nelson-Atkins Museum of Art – Kansas City, Missouri
3 Piedmont Park – Atlanta, Georgia
4 Minneapolis Sculpture Garden – Minneapolis, Minnesota
5 International Peace Garden – Dunseith, North Dakota

Who invented what

Text messages

Top Internet searches

Computer viruses

It won't work

SCIENCE
AND
TECHNOLOGY

Who invented what

Things are rarely invented just like that, out of the blue, with nothing or no-one having gone before, working along a similar path. And very often when the breakthrough comes, it's a team effort. Sometimes no-one knows the inventor, the original begetter never having been acknowledged, especially when the invention was a long time ago.

Here are some everyday, domestic objects in constant use, which we all roughly take for granted, with their probable origins.

FIVE INVENTIONS THAT TURN OUT TO BE INCREDIBLY ANCIENT

1 **Glass, 2500BC:** Could have been discovered by accident, when sand got heated with limestone and wood ash. Small glass ornamental beads have been found dating back to 2500BC, but it was the Egyptians around 1450BC who developed other uses, such as glass bottles.

2 **Locks, 2000BC:** The Egyptians used a wooden bolt held tight by pins dropped into holes – only a key shaped to push all the pins out of the way could open it. Much like locks today, really.

3 **Socks, 800BC:** The first wearers are not known, but presumably when we gave up bare feet for shoes of some sort, socks of some sort came in. The first mention of them was in a poem by the Greek poet Hesiod around 700BC. They were bits of felt at first, patched together. Knitted socks were created by the Egyptians around 450BC.

4 **Metal coins, 600BC:** People often exchanged a piece of precious metal for goods, but there was no standardised exchange value and it was hard to weigh and evaluate worth. The first known standardised coins, all weighing

the same, and stamped with the king's head, were issued around 600BC by the Lydians in what is now western Turkey.

5 **Central heating, 400BC:** The Romans brought central heating to Britain sometime after 43AD. You can see roughly how it worked in several bath houses in the Roman Forts on Hadrian's Wall – hot air was conducted along underfloor channels from a central charcoal-burning stove. They called the system 'hypocaust', which is Greek, suggesting perhaps the Greeks got there first. Hollow floors have been found in Greek ruins in Turkey.

FIVE REMARKABLY OLDISH INVENTIONS

1 **Spectacles, 1280AD:** A pair of glass lenses, clipped onto the nose, were first noted in the 13th century, but no inventor was credited. Spectacle-making was known in Florence from 1301 where Alessandro de Spina and Salvino degli Armatti were credited with inventing them. On the other hand, the Chinese say they got there first around 900AD.

2 **Watches, 1500:** Sundials or shadow clocks used to tell the time date from 3500. The origin of mechanical clocks, fitted into towers, is unknown, but the first striking clock was erected in Milan in 1335. Salisbury Cathedral had one from 1386 – it still works. Watches, which could be carried around, were invented by Peter Henlein, a German locksmith, in 1500. The original was about the size of a large mobile phone and was carried by hand.

3 **Pencil, 1565:** Invented by Conrad Gesner, a German–Swiss who realised the potential of graphite

and encased it in a wooden holder to form a means of writing.

4 **Flush lavatory, 1591**: John Harrington, an Elizabethan courtier, installed the first recorded one at Richmond Palace.

5 **Umbrella, 1637**: Louis XIII of France had one made of oiled cloth, for protection against the sun and rain. The first steel-ribbed opening umbrella was invented by an Englishman, Samuel Fox, in 1874.

EIGHT DEAD-MODERN INVENTIONS

1 **Jeans, 1873**: During the Gold Rush in the USA, Levi Strauss Co. supplied prospectors with materials and clothes, including trousers. A tailor called Jacob Davis suggested that trousers made of denim – a material that had originated from Nîmes in France, hence de Nîmes – complete with rivetted pockets, would go down well. And they did. In 1873 Strauss registered the first patent for jeans.

2 **Toothpaste, 1896**: As we know it, coming out of a tube, toothpaste was introduced by William Colgate in 1896. Before that it had been packaged in jars. It was tried in a tube in 1892 by another American, Washington Sheffield, but it didn't quite work. Colgate developed the tube nozzle so that the toothpaste, as it boasted on the side of the tube, 'comes out a ribbon, lies flat on the brush'.

3 **Safety razor, 1901**: Until then, men had shaved with open 'cut-throat' blades. King Camp Gillette invented a blade that fitted into a razor and was safe and also

disposable, which meant he sold millions. The first electric razor was also invented by an American – Col Jacob Schick of the US Army – who wanted to do away with wet shaving.

4 **Brassière, 1914**: New York partygoer Mary Jacob didn't like the feel of a whalebone corset under her new slinky dress and so chucked the whalebone and wore some handkerchieves tied with ribbon over her breasts. In 1914 she patented the brassière, later selling out to a major corset company.

5 **Tupperware, 1946**: Another amazing American invention; how would we have survived without it? Earl Tupper designed a plastic box with an airtight seal to be used in fridges – but at first no-one was much interested. Then he met ace saleswoman Brownie Wise. She suggested Tupperware parties – where hostesses demonstrated their use, then sold them. The Queen, who uses Tupperware at Buckingham Palace, will always be grateful.

6 **Velcro, 1950**: The name comes from the French for velvet, 'velours', and for hook, 'crochet'. Swiss inventor George de Mestral noticed how plant burrs clung to his dog, but it took him 15 years of research to find a way of creating the same effect.

7 **Mobile phone, 1970**: Pioneered in the USA by Bell Laboratories, they had a trial run in Chicago in 1979 and opened their first public service in 1983, but meanwhile the Scandinavians had got in first, launching their own system in 1981.

8 **World Wide Web, 1989**: Created by English physicist Tim Berners-Lee while working for the European

Centre for Nuclear Research in Switzerland. He needed to get information into computers scattered across the world; he defined the system, wrote the software, then passed it onto the world, for nothing. Thanks, Tim.

Text messages

Almost a third of mobile phone owners use text messaging to arrange their social lives. Many have dumped partners using a text, use it to arrange dates and to flirt. Others announce their children's birth via text, and/or use it to fire their employees.

According to youth culture researchers Roar, texting meets fundamental emotional and social needs by enabling young people to communicate secretly. It's also practical, affordable and personalised.

Popular texting

@wrk – at work

A/S – age/sex?

A3 – anytime, anywhere, anyplace

AB – ah, bless!

AFAIR – as far as I can remember/recall

Akcdnt – accident

AMBW – all my best wishes

AML – all my love

ASAP – as soon as f****** possible

ATT – about time too

AWCIGO – and where can I get one?

Grr – angry

RTcL – article

RUF2C – are you free to chat?

Top ringtones (Nokia, Sagem, Motorola and Ericsson phones)

Swing Low, Sweet Chariot

Clocks – Coldplay

Where is the love? – Black Eyed Peas

P.I.M.P – 50 cent feat. Snoop Dogg

Rhubarb & Custard

I believe in a thing called love

Rainbow

The Great Escape

Harry Potter – John Williams

Top Internet searches

Top Internet searches in the USA

Eight topics have appeared on the Lycos top Internet search list every week since August 1999, ranging from film stars to tattoos.

Pamela Anderson – film and TV star.

Dragonball – a show about intergalactic warriors.

Las Vegas – a popular city to search for, despite a temporary lapse in general searches for tourism and airlines after the 11 September attacks.

Jennifer Lopez – singer and film star.

Pokemon – Japanese cartoon; the only time it dropped from the Top 20 was the week of 11 September.

Britney Spears – teen popstar and the number one most searched term of 2000.

Tattoos – nearly half of all tattoo requests are incorrectly spelt.

WWF – the World Wrestling Federation.

Top searches of 2003
KaZaa

Harry Potter

'American Idol'

Britney Spears

50 Cent

Eminem

WWE (World Wrestling Entertainment)

Paris Hilton

NASCAR (car speeding sport)

Christina Aguilera

Top Internet searches in the UK:

With more and more people using the Internet to keep up with breaking news, search engines can provide a fast way of finding out latest developments. In 2003 AOL rated the following news stories as the most searched for:

Soham murders

Michael Jackson's arrest

John Leslie's arrest

The Iraq war

The SARS outbreak

In terms of sport, most people wanted to know about:

The Rugby World Cup

Wimbledon

The Ashes

The British Open

The FA Cup Final

And here are the celebrities most frequently entered into AOL search engines:

Male celebrities

David Blaine

Orlando Bloom

Johnny Depp

Justin Timberlake

David Beckham

Female celebrities

Christina Aquilera

Beyonce Knowles

Britney Spears

Barbie

Pamela Anderson

Computer viruses

The first computer virus appeared in 1986, five years after IBM introduced the PC and four years before the birth of the World Wide Web. However, a few years earlier Fred Cohen had already formally defined a computer virus as 'a computer program that can affect other computer programs by modifying them in such a way as to include a (possibly evolved) copy of itself.'

Newer infections spread faster than ever before, and at its peak the recent MyDoom worm was found in 1 in 9 messages transmitted globally. Here's a list of some of the earliest, most well-known or most dangerous computer viruses and worms:

1981	Apple 1, 2, and 3		Tristate
1987	Lehigh	2000	The Love Bug
1988	Jerusalem		The Stages
	MacMag	2001	Nimda
	Scores		Anna Kournikova
1991	Tequila		Sircam
1992	The Dark Avenger		CodeRed
	Mutation Engine		BadTrans
1994	Good Times	2002	Shakira
1995	Word Concept		Britney Spears
1996	Baza, Laroux and Staog		Jennifer Lopez
1998	StrangeBrew		Klez
	Chernobyl		Bugbear
1999	Melissa	2003	The Slammer
	Bubble Boy	2004	MyDoom

Source: www.Infoplease.com

It won't work

What they thought at the time. Look at them now...

Louis Pasteur's discoveries: 'It is absurd to think that germs causing fermentation and putrefaction come from the air; the atmosphere would have to be as thick as pea soup for that.' Dr Nicholas Joly, 1840.

Thomas Edison and electricity: 'Do not bother to sell your gas shares. The electric light has no future.' Professor John Henry Pepper.

George Stephenson and the opening of the Stockton–Darlington Railway, the world's first: 'What can be more palpably absurd and ridiculous than the prospect of locomotives travelling at twice the speed of stagecoaches.' *Quarterly Review*, 1825.

Aeroplanes: 'Artificial flight is impossible.' Professor Simon Newcomb, Director of the US Naval Observatory, 1894.

Alexander Graham Bell and the telephone: 'It is impossible to transmit speech electrically. The "telephone" is as mythical as the unicorn.' Professor Poggendorf, 1860.

Television: 'I showed them my invention for television. They evinced polite curiosity and then informed me that they were convinced that the transmission of images – especially mentioning fog as an impediment – was impossible.' John Logie Baird in a letter, 1940.

Space travel: 'In a sense, interplanetary travel is and remains utter bilge; the difficulties of setting up a launching station to arrange a safe return are enormous.' Dr Richard Woolley, Astronomer Royal, 1960.

The law and lawyers

Odd laws

Bizarre accidents

Americans' biggest worries

The UK's biggest worries

What we don't know

UFO sightings in north america

UFO sightings in the UK

SOCIETY

The law and lawyers

'The law is an ass,' said Mr Bumble in *Oliver Twist*. That was in fiction, but in real life Charles Dickens and many other worthies have had equally uncomplimentary things to say about our legal friends.

The Bible: 'Woe unto you lawyers, for you have taken away the key of knowledge.' St Luke, chapter 11, verse 52.

Cicero: 'The more laws, the less justice.'

Shakespeare: 'The first thing we do, let's kill all the lawyers.' *Henry VI*, part II.

Jonathan Swift: 'Laws are like cobwebs, which may catch small flies, but let wasps and hornets break through.'

Oliver Goldsmith: 'Laws grind the poor and rich men rule the law.'

Charles Dickens: 'The great principle of the English law is to make business for itself.'

Thomas Jefferson: 'It is the trade of lawyers to question everything, yield nothing, and talk by the hour.'

Franz Kafka: 'A lawyer is a person who writes a 10,000-word document and calls it a brief.'

Pierre Joseph Proudhon: 'Laws: we know what they are, and what they are worth. They are spider webs for the rich and mighty, steel chains for the poor and weak, fishing nets in the hand of the government.'

J.P. Morgan: 'I don't want a lawyer to tell me what I cannot do; I hire him to tell me how to do what I want to do.'

John Keats: 'I think we may class the lawyer in the natural history of monsters.'

Clarence Darrow: 'The law does not pretend to punish everything that is dishonest. That would seriously interfere with business.'

John Mortimer: 'No brilliance is required in law, just commonsense and relatively clean fingernails.'

Odd laws

If you've ever moved rhythmically to music in a premises with a liquor licence then you've broken the law – according to the Licensing Act of 1964. And according to a law passed in 1845, attempting to commit suicide was a capital offence. Offenders could be hanged for trying. Those laws applied to England, but here's a list of equally daft laws around the world:

Glasgow: It is illegal to be drunk and in possession of a cow

Bangkok: It is illegal to leave your house not wearing underwear

Victoria, Australia: Drivers can be fined for resting an arm out of the car window

Halifax, Canada: Wearing scented body products is banned

Athens, Greece: A driver's licence can be suspended if the driver is deemed either 'poorly dressed' or 'unbathed'

Quebec, Canada: Legally, margarine must be a different colour from butter

France: It is illegal to sell dolls that do not have human faces

HERE'S A RANGE OF DAFT USA LAWS

Alabama: It's illegal to wear a fake moustache that causes laughter in church

Fairbanks, Alaska: It is illegal to feed alcoholic beverages to a moose

San Francisco, California: It is illegal to wipe one's car with used underwear

Pueblo, Colorado: It is illegal to let a dandelion grow within city limits

Hartford, Connecticut: It is illegal to educate a dog

Florida: Unmarried women who parachute on Sundays may be jailed

Chicago, Illinois: It is illegal to fish in one's pyjamas

Massachusetts: It is illegal to duel with water pistols

Minnesota: Women can face up to 30 days in jail if they impersonate Santa Claus

Nebraska: It is illegal for a mother to give her daughter a perm without a state licence

Waterloo, Nebraska: Barbers are forbidden from eating onions between 7am and 7pm

New Jersey: It is illegal to 'frown' at a police officer

Youngstown, Ohio: It is illegal to run out of gas

Salt Lake City, Utah: It is illegal to carry an unwrapped ukulele on the street

Vermont: It is illegal to deny the existence of God

IN NEW YORK ALL THE FOLLOWING ARE ILLEGAL:

Smoking in public

Drinking alcohol in public

Feeding pigeons

Riding a bike with your feet off the pedals

Using mobile phones in cinemas

Ashtrays (except in private homes)

Variety of web and print sources, inc: www.members.tripod.com

Bizarre accidents in the UK

Nearly a million people a year end up in hospital after suffering bizarre accidents, estimated to cost around £1billion a year for treatment. Here are just some of them:

Contact with a non-powered hand-drill	3,038
Incidents with lawnmowers	369
Contact with plant thorns, spines, sharp leaves	190
Bitten or crushed by reptiles	51
Bitten by a rat	22

Source: Department of Health

Americans' biggest worries

Despite fears of terrorist attacks, Americans remain most anxious about finances and the death of loved ones, according to the Anxiety Disorders Association of America.

36% of people are 'very' or 'extremely' worried about their financial status

31% are anxious about a loved one dying

10% worry about their own death

Almost 50% have avoided people when feeling worried or anxious

Two in five have avoided answering their phones

For one in seven people, their worries have prevented them from leaving their homes.

The UK's Biggest worries

Londoners are the biggest worriers in the UK, repeatedly losing sleep over the well being of family members and hospital waiting lists. Concern about personal health and fitness also rates high on the list, as does the cost of living.

PERCENTAGE OF ADULTS WORRIED ABOUT:

Issue	London	UK
Family well-being	84	72
State of health service	82	80
Cost of living	82	70
Personal level of health/fitness	80	59
Way government runs the country	74	73
Financial well-being	74	73
Job satisfaction	73	52
Standard of living	72	48
State of British economy	72	63
Threat of terrorism	70	61
Neighbourhood crime	70	55
Local traffic	69	48
Immediate surroundings	69	48
Contact with family/friends	67	50
Personal stress levels	66	48
Local education facilities	64	44
Job security	64	51
Work/life balance	64	49
Saving the countryside	61	66
Investment climate, Britain	53	40
Level of noise where you live	52	30
Journey to work	48	26

Source: JPMorgan Fleming survey

What we don't know

Almost half of the British population has no idea who the deputy prime minister is, while many are convinced United Nations secretary general Kofi Annan is an Iraqi general.

Don't know deputy prime minister	47%
Embarrassed about general knowledge	12%

Source: study carried out for Whitaker's Almanack

UFO sightings in North America

One of the most commonly shaped UFOs reported to America's National UFO Reporting Center is a triangle, followed by a disk. But hardly anyone has sighted a dome or a pyramid.

The Center is located in Seattle, Washington, and was founded in 1974. It has a collection of UFO sightings dating as far back as 1860. The center's website has this disclaimer: 'The National UFO Reporting Center makes no claims as to the validity of the information in any of these reports. Obvious hoaxes have been omitted.'

The following is a list of some of the more common shapes reported over the years.

Shape	Number reported
Cigar	705
Circle	1945
Cone	121
Crescent	2
Cross	73
Cylinder	419
Diamond	401
Disk	2115
Dome	1

Egg	327
Fireball	1600
Flare	1
Flash	385
Hexagon	1
Light	4756
Oval	1073
Pyramid	1
Rectangle	351
Round	2
Sphere	1387
Teardrop	238
Triangle	2403

Your best chance of sighting an UFO in North America is in Washington and Texas. The list below shows the states with the highest number of reportings.

State	Sightings reported		
Arizona	909	New Jersey	427
British Columbia, Can.	443	Nevada	356
California	3191	New York	984
Colorado	521	Ohio	725
Florida	1019	Ontario, Can.	495
Georgia	355	Oregon	724
Illinois	729	Pennsylvania	676
Indiana	371	Tennessee	353
Massachusetts	360	Texas	1122
Michigan	632	Virginia	385
Missouri	500	Washington	1770
North Carolina	428	Wisconsin	447

UFO sightings in the UK

Residents of Lancashire and London report more UFO sightings than anywhere else in England, Scotland or Wales. The reports are posted on a UFO spotting website by 411 members, with the highest number of online users posting sightings on Christmas Eve…

Places with highest number of UFO sightings

England		Merseyside	27
Berkshire	15	Norfolk	22
Cheshire	14	West Yorkshire	22
Cornwall	17	*Scotland*	
Devon	15	Aberdeenshire	12
Essex	28	Lanarkshire	11
Hampshire	16	*Wales*	
Hertfordshire	15	Dyfed	9
Lancashire	36	Gwynedd	9
London	35	Mid Glamorgan	9

Other unusual sightings in the UK

The Blessed Virgin Mary:

Norfolk	11th century
Llanthony Monastery	1880
Middleton, Suffolk	1933

Weeping Madonna icon:

Newcastle upon Tyne	1955

Weeping crucifix:

Walthamstow, London	1966

Source: www.ufosightingsuk.co.uk and www.uktouristinfo.com

TRANSPORT
AND
TRAVEL

Journey times

When Sir Robert Peel was asked to become British prime minister in
1834 he was out of the country in Rome, Italy. He quickly set back to
England – a journey that took thirteen days.

While the use of rail rather than stagecoach slashed journey times
across Europe, there has been little change in the length of some British
train journeys over the past 100 years.

Route	Time in hours		
	1836 stagecoach	*1850 rail*	*1900 rail*
London–Birmingham	11	3	2½
London–Exeter	18	4¾	4
London–Liverpool	24	6½	4¼
London–Brighton	6	1¼	1¼
London–Edinburgh	43	12¼	8½

Source: Victorian life and transport, *Richard Dunning, 1981*

Worst train service in the UK

Only 70 per cent of long-distance trains in the UK arrive within 10
minutes of their scheduled time, with nearly 4 trains in 10 running late
in the Midlands. Midland Mainline operates the worst service, but
more than 1 in 3 Virgin West Coast and First Great Western trains also
arrive late. The best performers are Island Lines on the Isle of Wight
and Merseyrail.

Percentage of trains running on time

Long-distance operators	%
Anglia (inter-city)	76.6
Virgin Cross Country	68.3
GNER	67.9
First Great Western	65.8

Virgin West Coast	65.3
Midland Mainline	62.9

*London and south-east operators**	%
Chiltern	89.0
C2c	85.7
First Great Eastern	85.2
West Anglia Great Northern	82.5
South Central	81.0
Connex South Eastern	79.6
Silverlink	78.3
South West Trains	75.8
Thames Trains	74.7
Thameslink	68.6

* Trains in London and the south-east have to arrive within five minutes of their scheduled time to be regarded as on time.

Regional operators	%
Island Line	96.7
Merseyrail	94.2
Anglia (local)	88.1
ScotRail	87.0
Arriva Trains Northern	85.4
First North Western	82.8
Gatwick Express	81.8
Wales & Borders	81.1
Wessex Trains	80.8
Central Trains	72.9

*Source: the Strategic Rail Authority during
the period July–September 2003*

Excuses for train delays

The most popular excuse for a late train in the UK is the weather – be it snow, ice, leaves, wind or heat. Another common justification is the presence of something – or someone – on the line.

Here's an A to Z of less common excuses given for delays:

A drunk man on the line (Maidenhead, 1999)

Delayed due to the Royal Escort – the Royals can't be held up at any level crossing so the trains get delayed instead

Deranged female on the line (Leeds–Kings Cross train, north of Finsbury Park, 1994)

Driver abandons train

Driver having his tea break

Driver held up in motorway traffic

Due to no reason whatsoever (heard at Fleet)

Exploding pigeon (Kings Cross Thameslink)

Guard arrested for excess ticket fraud and taken away by police

Herons mating

Horse on the line

Overhanging tree branches (Market Harborough)

Person by the side of the line with a rifle

Portakabin blocking the line (between Watford Gap and Milton Keynes)

Rat self-destructed whilst chewing through signalling cables

Rugby-related problems (on Reading–Waterloo services after a rugby game at Twickenham)

Slippery rails all over the country (given at Surbiton)

Some Charlie's used an alarm handle as a coat hook (given on a London–Bedford Thameslink train)

The f****** train's broken down (given at Milton Keynes)

Train delayed due to Madonna (Liverpool Street, 1995 when Great Eastern held the last train of the evening to allow concert goers to return from Wembley)

Trainspotters on the line (near Grantham, 1999)

Source: www.rodge.force9.co.uk

Tube delays

If you've been stuck on a tube when the train suddenly stops – or been left standing waiting on a platform for a tube that never comes – then sometimes it's reassuring to be told the reason why, and sometimes not…

Tube announcements
'Ladies and gentlemen, I do apologise for the delay to your service. I know you're all dying to get home, unless, of course, you happen to be married to my ex-wife, in which case you'll want to cross over to the westbound and go in the opposite direction.'

'Your delay this evening is caused by the line controller suffering from E & B syndrome, not knowing his elbow from his backside. I'll let you know any further information as soon as I'm given any.'

'Do you want the good news first or the bad news? The good news is that last Friday was my birthday and I hit the town and had a great time. The bad news is that there is a points failure somewhere between Stratford and East Ham, which means we probably won't reach our destination.'

'Ladies and gentlemen, we apologise for the delay, but there is a security alert at Victoria station and we are therefore stuck here for the foreseeable future, so let's take our minds off it and pass some time together. All together now…"Ten green bottles, hanging on a wall…"'

'We are now travelling through Baker Street; as you can see Baker Street is closed. It would have been nice if they had actually told me, so I could tell you earlier, but no, they don't think about things like that.'

'Beggars are operating on this train, please do *not* encourage these professional beggars, if you have any spare change, please give it to a registered charity, failing that, give it to me.'

'Let the passengers off the train *first!*" [pause...] 'Oh go on then, stuff yourselves in like sardines, see if I care – I'm going home.'

'Please allow the doors to close. Try not to confuse this with "Please hold the doors open." The two are distinct and separate instructions.'

'Please note that the beeping noise coming from the doors means that the doors are about to close. It does not mean throw yourself or your bags into the doors.'

'We can't move off because some idiot has their effing hand stuck in the door.'

'To the gentleman wearing the long grey coat trying to get on the second carriage – what part of "stand clear of the doors" don't you understand?'

'Please move all baggage away from the doors. [pause...] Please move *all* belongings away from the doors. [pause...] This is a personal message to the man in the brown suit wearing glasses at the rear of the train – put the pie down, four-eyes, and move your bloody golf clubs away from the door before I come down there and shove them up your a**e sideways.'

'May I remind all passengers that there is strictly no smoking allowed on any part of the underground. However, if you are smoking a joint, it's only fair that you pass it round the rest of the carriage.'

Source: 'Skiver's Corner', BBC Lancashire

Top-selling vehicles in the USA

The most popular vehicle with American buyers is the full-size pickup truck. The following are the bestsellers for 2003:

Ford F-Series
Chevrolet Silverado
Dodge Ram
Toyota Camry
Honda Accord

Source: J.D.Power and Associates

Vehicle sales in the UK

According to a 2003 survey of car owners carried out by *What Car?* magazine, 13 of the 20 top cars in the UK are Japanese models. The top British car was the Coventry-built Jaguar XJ Series. The survey covered reliability, dealer service, running costs, ride and handling. The Volkswagen Sharan received just one star out of a possible five, making it the top worst car in the country.

The Top 10 best cars
Hondo Logo
Toyota Yaris
Lexus IS200
Jaguar XJ series
Smart City Coupe
Toyota Corolla
Skoda Octavia
Toyota Rav4
BMW 3-series
BMW 5-series

The Top 10 worst cars
VW Sharan
Chrysler Voyager
Alfa Romeo 156
MG Rover MGF
Ford Galaxy
Renault Espace
Fiat Punto
Fiat Bravo
Land Rover Freelander
Peugeot 307

The UK's favourite car colours

What does your car colour say about you? Well, if you drive a green car then you are more likely to have a driving conviction, according to the motor insurer Admiral. Red is popular among UK women drivers aged over 55, while surgeons favour silver cars and police officers purple.

Most popular UK car colours, 2002	Cars most likely to be stolen
Blue	White
Red	Black
Silver	Grey
White	Yellow
Green	Red

Source: Sunday Times, *Admiral, RAC Foundation*

North America's favourite car colours

Silver was North America's most popular car colour for 2003, according to DuPont Automotive. The following list shows the colour of cars produced in the USA and Canada in 2003; the numbers are said to provide a good indication of actual popularity.

Colour	Percentage of cars
Silver	20.2
White	18.4
Black	11.6
Medium/Dark grey	11.5
Light brown	8.8

Britain's most dangerous roads

The A537, a scenic route through the Peak District, is the most dangerous road in Britain, having been described by the European Road Assessment Programme as 'persistently high-risk'. The Programme identified 22 roads on which at least 1 person has been killed or seriously injured per mile in 3 years. Potentially lethal road hazards include trees, lampposts and telegraph poles – while the improvements that are needed include better junction layouts, signs and road markings, more barriers and speed cameras.

High-risk roads
A537, Macclesfield to Buxton
A534, Welsh boundary to Nantwich
A682, from the M65 junction 13 to the A65 at Long Preston
A54, from Congleton to Buxton
A631, from Gainsborough to the A1103
A683, from the A6 to Kirkby Lonsdale

Most stolen cars in USA

There were 1.2 million motor vehicle thefts in the USA in 2002, according to the National Insurance Crime Bureau. Its figures include cars that have parts removed or are taken for joyrides and later recovered.

Top 5 models for 2002
Toyota Camry
Honda Accord
Honda Civic
Chevrolet Full-Size Pickup
Ford Full-Size Pickup

Most stolen colour
White
Red
Blue
Black
Green

Source: MSN Autos

Dodgy insurance claims

Ever had an accident in the car that just *wasn't your fault*? So have these people...the following are said to be actual statements found on insurance claim forms where car drivers tried to sum up what happened to them:

'I told the police that I was not injured, but on removing my hat I found that I had a fractured skull.'

'I pulled away from the side of the road, glanced at my mother-in-law and headed over the embankment.'

'I thought my window was down, but I found it was up when I put my head through it.'

'I collided with a stationary truck coming the other way.'

'Coming home I drove into the wrong house and collided with a tree I don't have. The other car collided with mine without giving me warning of its intention.'

'A pedestrian hit me and went under my car.'

'The guy was all over the road. I had to swerve several times before I hit him.'

'In an attempt to kill a fly, I drove into a telephone pole.'

'I had been shopping for a plant all day and was on my way home. As I reached an intersection a hedge sprang up, obscuring my vision and I did not see the other car.'

'I was on the way to the doctor with rear end trouble when my universal joint gave way causing me to have an accident and damage my big end.'

'I had been driving for 40 years when I fell asleep at the wheel and had an accident.'

'As I approached the intersection a sign appeared in a place where no stop sign had ever appeared before. I was unable to stop in time to avoid the accident.'

'To avoid hitting the bumper of the car in front I struck a pedestrian.'

'My car was legally parked as it backed into another vehicle.'

'An invisible car came out of nowhere, struck my car and vanished.'

'I was sure the old fellow would never make it to the other side of the road when I struck him.'

'The telephone pole was approaching. I was attempting to swerve out the way when I struck the front end.'

'I saw a slow-moving, sad-faced old gentleman as he bounced off the roof of my car.'
'The indirect cause of the accident was a little guy in a small car with a big mouth.'

'The pedestrian had no idea which direction to run. So I ran over him.'

'The accident was caused by me waving to the man I hit last week.'

'I was thrown from my car as it left the road. I was later found in a ditch by some stray cows.'

'I knocked over a man; he admitted it was his fault as he'd been knocked over before.'

The finest hotels in the world

The following list comprises the hotels that *Tatler* magazine considers the finest in the world. It compiled a shortlist of 15 hotels for its 2003 Hotel of the Year Tatler Travel Awards.

Hotel	Cost
Chateau de Bagnols, Beaujolais	£300 to £840 per room per night
North Island, Seychelles	seven nights from £3,150 inc. flight
Oberoi, Mauritius	£350 to £500 per room per night
One Aldwych, London	£300 to £1000 per room per night
One & Only Le Touessrok, Mauritius	£400 to £500 per person per night
Barnsley House, Gloucestershire	£250 to £450 per room
Kurland, Plettenberg Bay, South Africa	from £140 per person per night
Elounda Gulf Villas, Crete	£105 to £1980 per room
Four Seasons, NYC and Beverly Hills	from £217 per person per night
Hotel Tresanton, St Mawes, Cornwall	£165 to £265 per room
The Standard, Downtown LA	£72 to £289 per person per night
Soho House, New York	$ 250 to $795 per room
Singita, Lebombo, South Africa	R6,625 per night
Taha'a Pearl beach, Tahiti	£380 to £520 per person per night
Vanyavilas, Rajasthan, India	£275 per person per night

Hotel notices

Ever seen a strange notice – in even stranger English – in a hotel room abroad? Here's a list of helpful tips found in European hotels:

DO NOT ENTER THE LIFT BACKWARDS,
AND ONLY WHEN LIT UP
(German hotel)

TO MOVE THE CABIN, PUSH BUTTON FOR WISHING
FLOOR. IF THE CABIN SHOULD ENTER MORE PERSONS,
EACH ONE SHOULD PRESS A NUMBER OF WISHING
FLOOR DRIVING IS THEN GOING ALPHABETICALLY BY
NATIONAL ORDER
(elevator in Belgrade hotel)

THE FLATTENING OF UNDERWEAR WITH PLEASURE IS
THE JOB OF THE CHAMBERMAID
(Yugoslavian hotel)

NOT TO PERAMBULATE THE CORRIDORS IN THE HOURS
OF REPOSE IN THE BOOTS OF ASCENSION
(Austrian hotel)

IN CASE OF FIRE, DO YOUR UTMOST TO ALARM THE
HOTEL PORTER
(Vienna hotel)

LADIES ARE REQUESTED
NOT TO HAVE CHILDREN IN THE BAR
(Norwegian hotel)

THIS HOTEL IS RENOWNED FOR ITS PEACE AND
SOLITUDE. IN FACT, CROWDS FROM ALL OVER THE
WORLD FLOCK HERE TO ENJOY ITS SOLITUDE
(Italian hotel brochure)

AND IN JAPAN:
GUESTS ARE REQUESTED NOT TO SMOKE
OR DO OTHER DISGUSTING BEHAVIOURS IN BED
(Tokyo hotel)

IS FORBIDDEN TO STEAL HOTEL TOWELS.
PLEASE IF YOU ARE NOT A PERSON TO DO SUCH A THING
IS PLEASE NOT TO READ NOTICE
(another Tokyo hotel)

COOLES AND HEATES: IF YOU WANT JUST CONDITION OF
WARM AIR IN YOUR ROOM, PLEASE CONTROL YOURSELF
(information booklet, Japanese hotel)

AS FOR SHOP AND OFFICE NOTICES:
LADIES HAVE FITS UPSTAIRS
(dress shop, Hong Kong)

ORDER YOUR SUMMERS SUIT BECAUSE IS BIG RUSH,
WE WILL EXECUTE CUSTOMERS IN STRICT ROTATION
(tailor shop, Rhodes)

LADIES, LEAVE YOUR CLOTHES HERE AND SPEND
THE AFTERNOON HAVING A GOOD TIME
(laundry in Rome)

FUR COATS MADE FOR LADIES
FROM THEIR OWN SKIN
(furrier in Sweden)

SPECIALIST IN WOMEN AND OTHER DISEASES
(doctor's office, Rome)

Source: variety of web sites

Travel tips

The following list is taken from travel websites that provide crucial tips for those travelling abroad:

Bangkok – go upstairs to Departures upon your arrival where you can get a cheaper taxi fare into the city

Jamaica – do not buy marijuana from anybody at the Kingston port or airport

Orlando – choose the left hand queue at Orlando theme parks, it will be shorter. Americans drive on the right hand side of the road and they all go for the right hand queue

Planes – the best economy seat on a 747 is the last one: there are only two seats in a three-seat area, it's close to the loos, you get fed and watered first

Russia – if you're travelling there in the summer, take plenty of mosquito spray

Safari – when camping or going on safari take a toilet roll with a string tied through the middle. This can be hung round your neck when visiting the loo, making it easily accessible and not likely to be dropped on wet/dirty floors

Singapore –take a small solar-powered calculator with you when you go shopping

Sri Lanka – please and thank you are not common words, it's done with a smile

South Africa – lock your car doors at all times because of car-hijacking

What to do – and not do – in Japan
Take your shoes off if you go into a Japanese house and leave them on the step outside
Take slip-on shoes, they are easier to get off than laces
Don't sit on a table
Don't put your shoes on a table or chair, even in the train
If you have to stand on a chair, take your shoes off first
If you have a problem with sweaty feet, use a foot deodorant
Don't hug or kiss
Don't call anyone by their first name.

Quotations on the USA

Things you were told as a child...

Things your parents said to you...

How to make your own luck

How to make people like you

Boy or girl? Predicting baby gender

Packing your labour bag for hospital

Good reasons not to get divorced

Things not to do during an interview

What not to say

What not to say to a Canadian abroad

WISDOMS
AND
ADVICE

Quotations on the USA

America's really only a kind of Russia
ANTHONY BURGESS, *Honey for Bears*

The business of America is business
CALVIN COOLIDGE 1925 speech

Whatever America hopes to bring to pass in this world
must first come to pass in the heart of America
PRESIDENT EISENHOWER, 1953 inaugural address

Dearest Alice, I could come back to America
(could be carried back on a stretcher) to die –
but never, never to live
HENRY JAMES in a letter to his sister-in-law Alice James

In the United States there is more space where nobody
is than where anybody is. That is what makes
America what it is
GERTRUDE STEIN, *The Geographical History of America*

Source: The Penguin Dictionary of Modern Quotations

Things you were told as a child and believed at the time

If the wind changes your face will stick like that.

Eat your crusts, it'll make your hair curly.

If you eat carrots you'll be able to see in the dark.

You'll catch cold if you go out with wet hair.

Eating spinach will make you strong.

If you swallow chewing gum, it'll stick your insides together.

If you sit on a stone step you'll get a chill in your kidneys.

If you squeeze it,
it'll never get better.

That'll put hairs on your chest.

If you eat the pips out of an apple you will get an apple tree growing from your tummy and out your ears.

If you fiddle with your belly button, your bum will unscrew.

Chewing gum is made of horse's hooves.

If you pick your nose, your head will cave in.

Things your parents said to you that you swore you'd never say to your own kids, but do...

Of course it won't hurt.

Because I said so!

Wait 'til your dad gets home!

We never had playstations/ mobile phones/shoes when we were young.

Eat your broccoli.

I never did that when
I was your age.

You don't know you're born.

No.

I remember when...

Haven't you grown?

Take your coat off so you'll feel the benefit of it when you go outside again.

You'll poke someone's eye out with that!

If you get run over I'll kill you.

Do you want a smack?

D'ya think I'm made o' money? You'll laugh on the other side of your face in a minute!

Do you think money grows on trees?

You'd look after it/them if you had to pay for it/them.

Don't look down the drain, 'cos you'll get scarlet fever.

If you pick at a spot it'll grow into a pig's foot.

You're not going out looking like that!

Put your coat on, you'll catch your death.

Wait till you have kids of your own

Make sure you've got clean underwear on, in case you get run over.

That's not music – it's just noise!

When I was your age…

How to make your own luck

Most people know it's lucky to find a four-leaf clover – but what about lucky elephant pictures?

A list of things to bring good luck
A horseshoe, hung above the doorway, will bring good luck to a home (some believe the horseshoe should be facing downward, others that it must be turned upward).

An acorn should be carried to bring luck and ensure a long life.

Spit on a new baseball bat before using it for the first time to make it lucky.

If a black cat walks towards you, it brings good fortune (but if it walks away, it takes the good luck with it).

Pictures of an elephant bring luck, but only if they face a door.

A list of things that could bring bad luck

Seeing an ambulance is very unlucky unless you pinch your nose or hold your breath until you see a black or a brown dog.

It's bad luck to put a hat on a bed.

Placing a bed facing north and south brings misfortune.

You must get out of bed on the same side that you get in or you will have bad luck.

If a bee enters your home, it's a sign that you will soon have a visitor. If you kill the bee, you will have bad luck, or the visitor will be unpleasant.

To drop a comb while you are combing your hair is a sign of a coming disappointment.

It's bad luck to leave a house through a different door than the one used to come into it.

It's bad luck to say the word 'pig' while fishing at sea.

To break a mirror means seven years bad luck

It's bad luck to close a pocket knife unless you were the one who opened it.

It's bad luck to let milk boil over.

Bad luck will follow the spilling of salt unless a pinch is thrown over the left shoulder into the face of the devil waiting there.

Do not place shoes upon a table, for this will bring bad luck for the day, cause trouble with your mate and you might even lose your job as a result.

Sparrows carry the souls of the dead, it's unlucky to kill one.

It's bad luck to open an umbrella inside the house, especially if you put it over your head.

A list of things not to do on a Friday

A bed changed on Friday will bring bad dreams.

Any ship that sails on Friday will have bad luck.

You should never start a trip on Friday or you will meet misfortune.

It is bad luck to cut your fingernails on Friday.

Never start to make a garment on Friday unless you can finish it the same day.

Source:www.corsinet.com

How to make people like you

Dale Carnegie, author of the 1930s blockbuster *How to win friends and influence people*, devised this list in order to help people make friends.

Six ways to make people like you
Rule 1: Become genuinely interested in other people.
Rule 2: Smile.
Rule 3: Remember that a man's name is to him the sweetest and most important sound in the English language.
Rule 4: Be a good listener. Encourage others to talk about themselves.
Rule 5: Talk in terms of the other man's interest.
Rule 6: Make the other person feel important – and do it sincerely.

And he compiled this helpful list for improving your home life:

Seven rules for making your home life happier
Rule 1: Don't nag.
Rule 2: Don't try to make your partner over.
Rule 3: Don't criticise.
Rule 4: Give honest appreciation.
Rule 5: Pay little attentions.
Rule 6: Be courteous.
Rule 7: Read a good book on the sexual side of marriage.

Boy or Girl? Predicting baby gender

Anyone who has been pregnant knows how much other people like guessing the sex of your unborn child. While modern tests like ultrasound and amniocentesis can spot the gender, here's a list of more traditional ways of playing the guessing game.

The following means it will be a boy
You carry high
The bump is all out at the front
The baby's heart rate is slow
The hair on your legs is growing faster during pregnancy
You are sleeping in a bed with your pillow to the north
Your feet are colder than they were before pregnancy
The father-to-be is gaining weight as well
The maternal grandmother has grey hair
Your urine is bright yellow
Your nose has been spreading
You have been craving meats or cheeses
You are looking particularly attractive during pregnancy
Your belly gets hairy
Your hands are dry and chapped

And these mean it will be a girl
You carry low
The bump is wide
Bad morning sickness
The baby's heart rate is fast (140 or more beats per minute)
You refuse to eat the crust of a loaf of bread
You had morning sickness early in pregnancy
Your breasts are dramatically increased during pregnancy
You are craving sweets
You get red highlights in your hair

Other ways for mothers-to-be to tell
Pick up a key. If you pick it up by the round end, it will be a

boy. If you pick it up by the long end, it will be a girl. And if you pick it up in the middle, you'll be having twins.

Hang a gold pendant over the palm of your hand. If the pendant moves in a circular fashion, it will be a girl. If it swings back and forth, it will be a boy.

The same goes for hanging a needle (or a wedding band) on a thread over your belly.

What side do you lie on while resting? On your left, it's boy, on your right, it's a girl.

Ask the mum-to-be to show her hands. If she shows them palm up it's a boy, palms down and it's a girl.

Various sources, including www.babycentre.co.uk, www.yourbaby.co.uk, www.smilechild.co.uk

Packing your labour bag for hospital

Pregnant women are advised to pack a bag with all the essentials towards the last two weeks of pregnancy in order to get ready for their hospital stay. BBC parenting advisors offer the following list of what to take with you for labour:

A clean t-shirt or front-opening nighties, dressing gown and slippers – plus bed socks if you have a tendency to get cold feet.

Maternity pads – night-time sanitary pads are fine – and knickers.

Drinks and snacks for you and whoever is going to be with you.

A small facial sponge, for dabbing and sucking on.

Body oil, fine talcum powder or lotion for back rubs.

Music tapes/CDs and a battery-operated player.

A hairband and brush, soap towel and flannel, toothbrush and paste, other toiletries as desired.

Other experts offer a more comprehensive list, including the following:
Your birth plan.

TENS machine plus spare batteries.

Aromatherapy oils to scent the room.

A fine water spray for cooling your face.

Lip salve.

A thermos of ice-cubes to suck on.

Hot-water bottle.
Slippers, in case you're pacing the corridors trying to encourage progress in a slow labour.

Spare shirt or t-shirt for your partner, it can be extremely hot in hospital. He may even want to change into shorts.

Bathing trunks for your labour partner if he is planning to physically support you in a birthing pool.

Special object to help you focus during labour.

Notebook in which to write a record of the labour – and a pen.

Camera.

Change or phone card for letting relatives and friends know the news.

Various sources, including www.babyworld.co.uk

Good reasons not to get divorced

The most common reasons for divorce are abuse and infidelity. But one relationship expert has come up with a list of the 10 most common reasons why people don't get divorced.

1 Loving one's spouse despite the spouse's serious shortcomings

2 Personal values – a staunch belief in the sanctity of marriage

3 Religious convictions

4 Limited financial resources or complex family financial entanglements

5 Worry that additional emotional damage will be inflicted on oneself, children and/or extended family

6 Fear of being a one-, two- or three-time divorce loser

7 Inconvenience of dismantling hearth and home

8 Poor health and lack of physical and emotional stamina

9 Fear of living alone

10 Ashamed of being considered a failure

Source: 'Should I stay or go? How controlled separation can save your marriage', *quoted on www.leeraffel.com*

Things not to do during an interview

The following list is provided by career's advice services in order to help interviewees.

1 Do not arrive late. You must allow enough time from when you leave your house to permit for unforeseen circumstances such as rail problems or traffic jams.

2 Do not fidget with items on the desk, or play with your hair and clothes.

3 Do not mumble, talk too fast, too softly or non-stop. Unless you speak clearly all of your sound comments will be lost on the interviewer and you will not impress.

4 Do not use slang words, crack silly jokes or chew gum.

5 Do not lean on the interviewer's desk or frequently glance at your watch.

6 Do not hide any aspect of your previous record, overstate qualifications, brag or get angry.

7 Do not call the interviewer by his/her first name, or become involved in any negative aspect of your current employer, classes or university.

8 Do not show ignorance about the company – allow your research to come through in conversation.

9 Do not appear half-asleep; go to bed early the night before the interview and sleep soundly knowing that you are fully prepared for the day ahead.

10 Do not bring up the topic of salary. When the time is right, salary will be discussed.

11 If it is an interview over lunch, do not order the spaghetti.

12 Do not come across as being passive or indifferent, be positive and enthusiastic.

13 Do not be overbearing or conceited.

14 Be friendly and open, but do not flirt with the interviewer.

15. Do not use negative body language, or convey inappropriate aspects of your character.

Most importantly:
16. Do not ask to see the interviewer's resume to see if they are qualified to judge you as a candidate.

17. Do not over-emphasise your ability to use a photocopier.

18. Do not, upon walking into the office for the first time, ask the receptionist to hold all your calls.

19. Do not explain that your long-term goal is to have the interviewer's job.

What not to say

What not to say to a police officer when you get pulled over:
I can't reach my licence unless you hold my beer.

Sorry, officer, I didn't realise my radar detector wasn't plugged in.

Aren't you the guy from the Village People?

Hey, you must have been doing about 125mph to keep up with me! Well done!

I thought you had to be in relatively good physical condition to be a police officer?

What not to say to a reporter:
This is off the record – the reporter will now carefully note everything you say and reproduce it, to your acute embarrassment.

I've never heard of your magazine/radio show/TV programme – local reporters grow up to be national reporters so treat them well.

This afternoon? Don't be ridiculous, we're not working to your deadlines – the media is driven by deadlines, this is a good way to guarantee no publicity or bad publicity.

No comment – you will then be quoted as declining to confirm or deny rumours, or you'll be described as refusing point blank to talk.

I think I could let you have one of these free (wink) – don't try to buy publicity with bribes, it could backfire.

Source: mediacoach website

What not to say to a Canadian abroad

The following list was compiled by www.thecanadapage.org as some of the most annoyingly frequent statements made to Canadians living abroad.

So…it's like cold there, right?

Who is your president?

You're from Canada. Do you know [so and so] from [random Canadian city]?

Aren't you guys British?

Do you like Bryan Adams?

Hey! I saw [random Canadian actor/singer] on TV yesterday! And he's Canadian – I was going to call you.

Can you say aboot for me? Eh?

So when are you guys going to join the US?

Hard words

Top 10 words of 2003 in the USA

Acronyms

You say tomatoes...

American mountain biking slang

Children's slang

Doctor's slang

Australian cant

Australian drinking terms

Anti-Iraq war slogans

Things you can't help saying...

Famous last words

Epitaphs

WORDS

Hard words

The *Oxford Dictionary of Synonyms and Antonyms* has, at the end of the book, 85 pages of what they call 'A lexicon of Hard Words'. Just in case at this very moment you should be playing Scrabble, and are desperate for a word beginning with A or perhaps Z, to confound your opponent, here are the first five and last five in their invaluable lexicon.

A

aam – a former liquid wine measure of 37 to 41 gallons; a cask

abatia (also **abattis**) – a defence made of felled trees with the boughs pointing outwards

abecedarian – 1) one occupied in learning the alphabet. – 2) a teacher of the alphabet

aberdevine – a bird-fancier's name for the siskin, a small bird like a goldfinch

aberrant – diverging from the normal type or accepted standard

Z

ziggurat – a rectangular stepped tower in ancient Mesopotamia, with a temple on top

zillah – an administrative district in India

zoetrope – an old-fashioned optical toy in the form of a picture-lined cylinder producing moving images when revolved and viewed through a slit

zymosis – fermentation

zymurgy – the branch of applied chemistry dealing with the use of fermentation in brewing etc.

Top 10 words of 2003 in the USA

Your.Dictionary.com has compiled lists of the top words, phrases and youth speak of 2003. The lists feature words that made the news in the United States last year, with many originating from the war in Iraq.

Top 10 words
Embedded
Blog
SARS
Spam
Taikonaut
Bushism
Allision
Recall
Middangeard
Celibacy

Top 10 youthspeak
What up?
Give it up!
Shut up!
Stog (cigarette)
SNAG (Sensitive New Age
    Guy)
Hottie

Poppins (meaning 'perfect')
Tricked Out (souped up)
Rice Rockets (tricked out
    Japanese compact cars)
Side Show (temporarily
    cordoning off a freeway to
    perform car stunts in
    tricked out rice rockets)

Top 10 phrases
Shock-and-Awe
Rush to War
Tire Pressure
Weapons of Mass Destruction
16 Words
Guantanamo Bay
Spider-Hole
Tipping Point
Angry Left
Halliburton Energy Services

Acronyms

Many of the acronyms below originated from the 1980s, when they were popular terms used in marketing or advertising, except for TIRED, which is a 21st-century invention.

Tired: Thirtysomething Independent Radical Educated Dropout
Yuppies: Young Urban Professionals
Yummies: Young Urban Mothers
Dinkies: Double Income No Kids
Sinkies: Single Income No Kids
Sitcom: Single Income Two Children Oppressive Marriage
Minkie: Middle Income No Kids
Poupie: Porsche-Owning Urban Professional
Swell: Single Woman Earning Lots of Loot (Miss Yuppie)
Guppies: Greenpeace Yuppies
Bobo: Burnt Out But Opulent
Empty Nesters: Couples whose children are grown up and away
Woopie: Well Off Older People
Jollies: Jet-Setting Oldsters with Lots of Loot
Glams: Greying Leisured Affluent Middle-Aged
Deccie: D.I.Y. Decorators Who Drag, Stipple and Marble
Splappie: Stripped Pine Laura Ashley People
Drabbie: Ethical urban quaker with anti and pro views
Dockney: East Docklands London Yuppie
Tweenie: Between 5 and 12 years old
Ladettes: Young women who act like loutish lads
Grey Panthers: Senior citizens with opinion

You say tomatoes...

Americans and Brits may speak the same English language – but what we call one thing, they call another. Here's a list:

UK	USA
sweets	candy
aubergine	eggplant
bap	sandwich roll
biscuit	cookie
bramble	(wild) black raspberry
cakes	pastries
candy floss	cotton candy
cornflour	cornstarch
courgette	zucchini
crisps	potato chips
chips	French fries
iced lollies/lollipops	popsicles
jacket potato	baked potato
jelly	gelatin (Jell-O)
ladyfingers	okra (also bhindi)
mange-tout	snow peas
muesli	granola
off-licence/offie	liquor store
sultana	golden raisins
swede	rutabaga
wholemeal	whole-wheat

American mountain biking slang

You're wearing your brain bucket and you're nicely dialed in, when you suddenly have a close encounter with a banana scraper and end up bonked and about to honk. Which sport are you enjoying?

Slang terms used in mountain biking often come from the off-road motorcycling culture, while many of the terms for 'crash' came from skiing, snowboarding, surfing or skating. The following is a selection of slang terms taken from the online slang dictionary.

acro-brat *n.* little kids who use their bikes like pogo sticks, with pegs coming out of the front axle.

bacon *n.* scabs on a rider's knees, elbows or other body parts.

bag *v.* to fail to show. 'Tom swore he'd be there but he bagged.'

banana scraper *n.* low-hanging branches.

biff *n.* a crash.

bonk *v.* to run out of energy or grow exhausted on a ride. 'I bonked so early it was embarrassing.'

brain bucket *n.* helmet.

brain sieve *n.* a helmet featuring more vents than protective surface.

bring home a Christmas tree *v.* to ride (or crash) through dense bushes, so leaves and branches are hanging from your bike and helmet.

chi-chi *n.* extravagant parts used to dress up a bicycle to make it more impressive looking.

clotheslined *v.* the act of catching an upper body part (*e.g.* the neck) on a low piece of vegetation, resulting in separation of the rider from the bike.

death cookies *n.* fist-sized rocks that knock your bike in every direction but the one you want to proceed in.

dialed in *adj.* when a bike is set up nicely and everything works just right.

endo *n.* the manoeuvre of flying unexpectedly over the handlebars, thus being forcibly ejected from the bike. Short for 'end over end'.

gonzo *adj.* treacherous, extreme. 'That vertical drop was sheer gonzo.'

gnarl *n.* extreme technical sections. Characterised by very rough, rooty, slippery or rocky sections.

gravity check *n.* a fall.

hamburger *n.* the condition of skin when geological contact was made with sharp rocks.

honk *v.* to vomit due to cycling exertion.

impedimentia *n.* all the junk on a bike that impedes performance *and* looks bad.

John boy'ed *v.* when a rider's face gets covered with spots of mud, making him look like 'John Boy' on the Waltons. 'I hit that mudhole and got John boy'ed big time.'

kack *n.* an injury to the shin received while doing trials, a kack can be the result of any injury received during technical riding.

mud-ectomy 1) *n.* a shower after a ride on a muddy trail. 2) *v.* the act of becoming clean.

nosepickium *n.* the crusties you pick from your nose after a ride in a dusty environ.

Pirelliology *n.* the noble art of being able to identify tyres from the tracks they leave on the ground.

potato chip *n.* a wheel that has been badly bent.

retro-grouch *n.* a rider who prefers an old bike with old components and isn't fond of new, high-tech equipment.

Ride On! *n.* a parting phrase used by riders without much else to say.

rock-ectomy *v.* removing rocks, dirt, gravel from one's person.

tea party *n.* when a whole group of riders stops and chats, and nobody seems to want to ride on.

tombstone *n.* one of those little rocks protruding out of the trail that you don't notice because you are having a heart attack climbing the hill.

trail mix *n.* the involuntary release of last night's dinner by the way it came in.

unobtanium *adj.* describing a bike or accessory made from expensive, high-tech material. A play on 'unobtainable' and 'titanium'.

void *n.* 1) to empty the contents of one's bladder. 2) a deep chasm that you have to clear or you will die.

whoop-de-doos *n.* a series of up-and-down bumps, suitable for jumping.

wild pigs *n.* poorly adjusted brake pads that squeal in use.

winky *n.* a reflector.

The Zone *n.* a state of mind experienced while riding. You don't think, you just do.

Children's slang

What were you at school – a sprag or a hermit?

Sprag – one who tells a grown-up about other children's misdemeanors

Anchor – siblings or other small kids who keep you from going out with your mates

Exypesh – extremely special

Ming-ray – to tip the contents of someone's unattended satchel across the playground

Hermit – hopeless footballer who stands still during matches and never touches the ball

Sag off – play truant

Scabber – someone who tries to borrow money, food or PE kit from others

Sesh – cool, very satisfactory

Source: The Dictionary of Playground Slang, *Chris Lewis, 2003*

Doctor's slang

British doctors don't just have illegible handwriting, they also jot down insulting acronyms about their patients and colleagues. The increasing rate of litigation means there's a higher chance they will have to explain their notes in court, which means doctor slang is now becoming a dying art. Defenders argue that morbid humour and euphemism is a way of coping with daily exposure to injury, death and disease.

Doctor slang for imminent death
CTD – circling the drain, patient expected to die soon
GPO – good for parts only
AGMI – ain't gonna make it

Descriptions of patients
NFN – normal for Norfolk
FLKOFS – funny looking kid, okay for Sunderland
SWW – sick, wet, whiny (infant)
OAP – over-anxious patient
LOFD – looks okay from door

Common afflictions
AGA – acute gravity attack (fell over)
PFO – drunk (pissed) and fell over
PGT – drunk and got thumped
WW1 – walking while intoxicated
NPS – new-parent syndrome
FABIANS – felt awful but I'm alright now syndrome

Advice given
TEETH – tried everything else, try homeopathy
PRATFO – patient reassured and told to f*** off

Sources: http.//news.bbc.co.uk, www.shartwell.freeserve.co.uk

Australian cant

The following is a list of underworld vocabulary used by white convicts in Australia in the early 1800s. Many of the terms hailed originally from English prisons.

Bash – to beat
Blow the gaff – to reveal a secret
Bounce – to bully
Cheese it! – stop it!
Dollop – a large quantity of anything
Kid – to deceive
Mizzle – to run away
Office – a hint or signal
School – a number of persons met together to gamble
Up the spout – in pawn

The following words, on the other hand, are often thought of as being English, but were first recorded in Australia.

Word	Australian date	English date
Bike	1869	1890
Chance it	1835	1933
Chain gang	1840	1858
Down under	1900	1908
Paralytic (drunk)	1890	1910
Yum yum	1883	1904

After the First World War words ending with the -o suffix became increasingly popular in Australia. The suffix was often tacked on to place names, and to certain lines of businesses, as in the following list:

Afto – afternoon
Beddo – bed
Bombo – cheap wine
Bottle-o – a bottle collector

Botto – bottle
Bronzo – the anus
Bullo – nonsense
Cacko – very drunk
Cazo – a war casualty
Cobbo – a friend or companion
Confo – conference
Commo – a communist
Compo – worker's compensation
Demo – demonstration
Evo – evening
Garbo – a garbage collector
Jello – jealous
Journo – journalist
Lavo – lavatory
Oppo – opportunity
Pendo – appendix
Prego – pregnant
Salvo – member of the Salvation Army
Sango – sandwich
Spello – rest or break in work

And here are some of the more colourful Australian metaphors

Buzz around like a blue-arsed fly
Like a duck in a ploughed paddock
Cold enough to freeze the balls of a billiard table
Mopey as a wet hen
Dull as a month of Sundays
So poor he's licking paint off the fence
As free from sense as a frog from feathers
Weaker than a sun-burned snowflake

Source: The Australian Language, *Sidney J. Baker, first published 1945*

Australian drinking terms

Slang terms for drunks
Beer swipers
Booze artists
Booze hounds
Booze kings
Boozicians
Boozingtons
Caterpillars
Leanaways
Slurks
Tids
Swippingtons
Jobs
Lolly legs
Shicks

A person who is drunk is said to be:
Blithered
Plonked up
Rotten
Molo
Molly
Stinko
Full as a bull's bum
Half-rinsed
Half-cut
Snockered
Inked
Inkypoo
Pinko
In the grip of the grape

Slang used in the 1960s for drinking and drinking bouts
Session
Rort
Beer-up
Booze-up
Break-out
Drunk-up
Grog-up
Jamberoo
Jollo
Perisher
Shivoo
Shiveroo
To go on the scoot
To tip the little finger

Anti-Iraq war slogans

The following is a list of slogans used on the 2003 British marches against the Iraq war.

Fighting for peace is like screwing for chastity
Stop mad cowboy disease
Smart bombs don't justify dumb leaders
War is so 20th century
Don't mess with Mesopotamia
Lets try pre-emptive peace
All humanity is downwind
Lies, damned lies and dodgy dossiers
Read between the pipelines
How did our oil get under their sand?

Things you can't help saying, yet know are really annoying...

Fans of the BBC Lancashire web site compiled a list of really annoying things that despite best intentions they still find themselves saying.

1 You know what I mean?

2 At the end of the day...

3 Like

4 I'm not being horrible, but...

5 It'll all come out in the wash

6 Whatever

7 If I were you...

8 I'll tell you what

9 Ooh...er...missus

10 Thingy, wotsit

11 I wouldn't do that if you paid me

12 This, that and the other

13 Etc.

14 So on and so forth

15 Absolutely

16 Erm

17 I won't tell you again, listen

Source: 'Skiver's Corner', a feature of the BBC Lancashire website,
www.bbc.co.uk/lancashire/fun

Famous last words

From those scared to go, to those who couldn't wait, here's a list of what the famous reportedly said in their last breath:

This is the last of earth! I am content.
JOHN QUINCY ADAMS, US President, d. 23 February, 1848

Is it not meningitis?
LOUISA M. ALCOTT, writer, d. 6 March, 1888

Waiting are they? Waiting are they? Well – let 'em wait.
In response to an attending doctor who attempted to comfort him by saying, *'General, I fear the angels are waiting for you.'*
ETHAN ALLEN, American Revolutionary general, d. 12 February, 1789

Am I dying or is this my birthday?
When she woke briefly during her last illness and found all her family around her bedside.
LADY NANCY ASTOR, d. 2 May, 1964

Nothing, but death.
When asked by her sister, Cassandra, if there was anything she wanted.
JANE AUSTEN, writer, d. 18 July, 1817

How were the receipts today at Madison Square Garden?
P.T. BARNUM, entrepreneur, d. 7 April, 1891

I can't sleep.
JAMES M. BARRIE, author, d. 19 June, 1937

Is everybody happy? I want everybody to be happy. I know I'm happy.
ETHEL BARRYMORE, actress, d. 18 June, 1959

Now comes the mystery.
HENRY WARD BEECHER, evangelist, d. 8 March, 1887

Friends applaud, the comedy is finished.
LUDWIG VAN BEETHOVEN, composer, d. 26 March, 1827

I should never have switched from Scotch to Martinis.
HUMPHREY BOGART, actor, d. 14 January, 1957

Ay Jesus.
CHARLES V, King of France, d. 1380

*I am about to – or I am going to –
die: either expression is correct.*
DOMINIQUE BOUHOURS, French
grammarian, d. 1702

Beautiful.
In reply to her husband who had
asked how she felt.
ELIZABETH BARRETT BROWNING,
writer, d. 29 June, 1861

I am still alive!
Stabbed to death by his own
guards (as reported by Roman
historian Tacitus).
GAIUS CALIGULA, Roman
Emperor, d. 41AD

I'm bored with it all.
Before slipping into a coma.
He died nine days later.
WINSTON CHURCHILL, statesman,
d. 24 January, 1965

*Damn it…Don't you dare ask God
to help me.*
To her housekeeper, who had
begun to pray aloud.
JOAN CRAWFORD, actress,
d. 10 May, 1977

My God. What's happened?
DIANA (SPENCER), Princess of
Wales, d. 31 August, 1997

I must go in, the fog is rising.
EMILY DICKINSON, poet,
d. 15 May, 1886

*Please know that I am quite aware
of the hazards. Women must try
to do things as men have tried.
When they fail, their failure must
be but a challenge to others.*
Last letter to her husband before
her last flight.
*KHAQQ calling Itasca. We must be
on you, but cannot see you.
Gas is running low.*
Last radio communiqué before
her disappearance.
AMELIA EARHART,
disappeared 2 July, 1937

*All my possessions
for a moment of time.*
ELIZABETH I, Queen of England,
d. 1603

I've never felt better.
DOUGLAS FAIRBANKS, SR, actor,
d. 12 December, 1939

*Turn up the lights, I don't want to
go home in the dark.*
O. HENRY (WILLIAM SIDNEY
PORTER), writer, d. 5 June, 1910

I see black light.
VICTOR HUGO, writer,
d. 22 May, 1885

Let's cool it, brothers…
Spoken to his assassins, 3 men
who shot him 15 times.
> MALCOLM X, Black leader,
> d. 21 February, 1965

Go on, get out – last words are for
fools who haven't said enough.
To his housekeeper, who urged
him to tell her his last words so
she could write them down for
posterity.
> KARL MARX, revolutionary,
> d. 14 March, 1883

Nothing matters. Nothing matters.
> LOUIS B. MAYER, film producer,
> d. 29 October, 1957

It's all been very interesting.
> LADY MARY WORTLEY MONTAGU,
> writer, d. 21 August, 1762

I knew it. I knew it. Born in a hotel
room – and God damn it – died
in a hotel room.
> EUGENE O'NEILL, writer,
> d. 27 November, 1953

I've had eighteen straight whiskies,
I think that's the record…
> DYLAN THOMAS, poet,
> d. 9 November, 1953

Get my swan costume ready.
> ANNA PAVLOVA, ballerina,
> d. 23 January, 1931

I love you, Sarah. For all eternity,
I love you.
Spoken to his wife.
> JAMES K. POLK, US President,
> d. 1849

I owe much; I have nothing; the rest
I leave to the poor.
> FRANÇOIS RABELAIS, writer, d. 1553

They couldn't hit an elephant at
this dist…
Killed in battle during
US Civil War.
> GENERAL JOHN SEDGWICK, Union
> Commander, d. 1864

Woe is me. Me thinks I'm turning
into a god.
> VESPASIAN, Roman Emperor,
> d. 79AD

Go away. I'm all right.
> H.G. WELLS, novelist,
> d. 13August, 1946

Either that wallpaper goes, or I do.
> OSCAR WILDE, writer,
> d. 30 November, 1900

Source: www.corsinet.com

Epitaphs

Some epitaphs, taken from gravestones in the United States and the UK, are worth remembering for their wit or wisdom, even though the people concerned might be long forgotten.

On the grave of Ezekial Aikle in
East Dalhousie Cemetery, Nova Scotia

Here lies
Ezekial Aikle
Age 102
The Good
Die Young.

In a cemetery in London, England

Here lies Ann Mann,
Who lived an old maid
But died an old Mann.
Dec. 8, 1767

In a Ruidoso, New Mexico, cemetery

Here lies
Johnny Yeast
Pardon me
For not rising.

In a Silver City, Nevada, cemetery

Here lays Butch,
We planted him raw.
He was quick on the trigger,
But slow on the draw.

A lawyer's epitaph in England

Sir John Strange
Here lies an honest lawyer,
And that is Strange.

Someone determined to be
anonymous in Stowe, Vermont
I was somebody.
Who, is no business
Of yours.

A widow wrote this epitaph in a Vermont cemetery
Sacred to the memory of
my husband John Barnes
who died January 3, 1803.
His comely young widow, aged 23, has
many qualifications of a good wife, and
yearns to be comforted.

In a Georgia cemetery
I told you I was sick!

In a cemetery in Hartscombe, England
On the 22nd of June
Jonathan Fiddle –
Went out of tune.

Someone in Winslow, Maine didn't like Mr Wood
In Memory of Beza Wood
Departed this life
Nov. 2, 1837
Aged 45 yrs.
Here lies one Wood
Enclosed in wood
One Wood
Within another.
The outer wood
Is very good:
We cannot praise
The other.

Owen Moore in Battersea, London, England
Gone away
Owin' more
Than he could pay.

On a grave from the 1880s in Nantucket, Massachusetts
Under the sod and under the trees
Lies the body of Jonathan Pease.
He is not here, there's only the pod:
Pease shelled out and went to God.

The grave of Ellen Shannon in Girard, Pennsylvania
Who was fatally burned
March 21, 1870
by the explosion of a lamp
filled with 'R.E. Danforth's
Non-Explosive Burning Fluid'

In a Thurmont, Maryland, cemetery
Here lies an Atheist
All dressed up
And no place to go.

Dr Fred Roberts, Brookland, Arkansas
Office upstairs.

In Newbury, England (1742)
Tom Smith is dead, and here he lies,
Nobody laughs and nobody cries;
Where his soul's gone, or how it fares,
Nobody knows, and nobody cares.

The Tired Woman's Epitaph
Here lies a poor woman who was always tired;
She lived in a house where help was not hired.
Her last words on earth were: "Dear friends, I am going
Where washing ain't done, nor sweeping, nor sewing:
But everything there is exact to my wishes;
For where they don't eat there's no washing of dishes...
Don't mourn for me now; don't mourn for me never –
I'm going to do nothing for ever and ever.

To the Memory of Abraham Beaulieu
Born 15 September 1822
Accidentally shot
4th April 1844
As a mark of affection
from his brother.

On an innkeeper (1875)
Beneath this stone, in hopes of Zion,
Doth lie the landlord of the Lion;
His son keeps on the business still,
Resigned unto the heavenly will.

Source: www.blakjak.demon.co.uk

**The first printed
shopping list**

**Online museum of
shopping lists**

**Too listless
to make lists?**

**A list of 10 things to do
after reading this book**

LISTS
ABOUT
LISTS

Finally, for those interested in lists, just as lists, the art of, the collection of, not really for their content, just for their very wonderful existence, here are three jolly interesting lists.

The first printed shopping list

There's no proof of this, but we like to think that in the first edition of this book, back in 1980, we printed what could well have been the first shopping list to appear in a non-fiction book – in novels they had been used long before that – and revealed the existence of the first known collector of shopping lists. OK, the first we had ever known about. A Mrs Louise Gill from Devon wrote to tell us how it all began.

Exeter, Devon, 20 January 1980.

Dear Mr Davies,

In my college days I began a scrapbook of lists, collected on pavements, in library books and on supermarket floors. These lists were mostly shopping lists, probably the lists most often written in everyday life, especially by women. This collection consisted of lists written on various articles, from old Christmas cards to torn-out diary pages. I now have a collection of 60 shopping lists in my scrapbook.

This is the very first list I acquired, found on a café table complete with the biro, in the summer of 1974 at the Princess Pavilion, Falmouth, Cornwall – now called the Tivoli Biergarten. It is certainly an odd mixture of items!

½ yd orange velvet velcro (green or lilac)
12 lemon squeezers
Body Language bra 36A
Dress
My necklace
Prescription
Bar of Old English Lavender soap
Records
Mincemeat

Online museum of shopping lists

Ever wondered what happened to the shopping list you scribbled on an old envelope last week and which has since disappeared? One answer could be it was picked up from the supermarket floor, scanned, and sent to the world's first Online Museum of Shopping Lists.

The web site is for everyone who is curious about what other people shop for, and those who believe the shopping list is a dying art. To the website owners, the shopping list 'represents a symbol of our vanishing individuality as we grow daily more uniform, passive and accepting'. While you can easily discover what people have bought by studying their till receipts, 'the list they have written before going out to the shops tells you about what they want and what they think they might need'.

Among the online shopping list exhibits are:
> Bleach
> White bin liners
> Black bags
> Dog collar
> Ariel liquid
> Bubble bath
> Shower gel – pink
> Car
> Clothes pegs
> Mouthwash
> Radio-controlled car

Things we need for the house (all as written)
> Pine Soul
> Papper towels
> Toilet papper
> Detergent liquet
> Dishwash liquet
> Forbreeze
> Shampoo/conditioner

Soup
Pads (for me)
Get money order for $23.14
One Electric bill
$8.00 birth certificate

Too listless to make lists?

There is also a web site, www.lifesaverlists, that will help you compile lists, if you are too tired, too bored or too listless to bother doing your own. They have an array of ready-made lists, on a variety of topics, to help you, for example, when you're about to go out shopping. The site also promises to act as 'your personal organiser' for small daily tasks, holiday planning or big celebrations. The web site even offers tips about how to look after our lists, so that you can use them again. Well, you wouldn't want to muck them up, would you?

Their top list tip is as follows: 'After printing out your list, place it in a plastic sleeve and use a dry-erase marker to check off items from the list as necessary. When finished using your list, simply wipe the sleeve clean with a tissue and the list is instantly reusable!'

We put in two topics, just to see what sort of stuff they would list for us, one on pampered pets and the other on what to put in your gym bag.

The pampered pet
Everything your pampered pet needs:
Toenail clippers (keep them sharp)
Sharp scissors (trimming fur from pads of feet)
Quality shampoo for dogs (for colour and non-drying for skin)
Toothbrush and toothpaste
Leash and collar
Chew toy (so they don't chew your toys)
Nutritious snacks or 'treats'
Brushes and combs (brush for coat/comb for skin)
'Splat mat' for under the food and water bowls

What to put in your gym bag
Towel & facecloth
Large bath towel
Body poof
Deodorant
Baby powder
Body and facial cleansers
Moisturizers (face and body)
Shampoo and conditioner
Brush and comb
Flip-flops for in the shower
Hairdryer
Cosmetics
Bathing suit
Swimming goggles
Nose plugs
Extra t-shirt
Extra sweatshirt
Extra socks
Extra tack pants
Shorts
Bottled water
Energy bar
Sweatbands

A list of 10 things to do
after reading this book

1   Pay for it. Especially if you have been standing for two hours in a bookshop reading it. You mean thing. Publishers and booksellers have to live.

2   Get it out again. That's if you have borrowed it from the library. There is a system called PLR – Public Lending Right – whereby authors get a small amount of money based on a random sample of library borrowings. Authors, too, have a right to live.

3   Tell all your friends how excellent, amusing, informative it was.

4   Even if you haven't quite finished. Or even got halfway.

5   Buy several copies. You can already tell it will make a first-class birthday, Christmas, special present for all ages, all types, so why not get it now, before you forget.

6   Don't write in with any spelling mistakes, literals or other mistakes you have spotted. Boring, boring.

7   If, of course, there are any, which is highly unlikely.

8   Anyway, we're bound to have caught them by now.

9   But do write in if you have any favourite lists, of any sort, which you have created or spotted somewhere. If we use them in the next edition of the book, your name will be credited and a uniformed messenger, i.e. postman, will deliver a free copy of the book to your door.

10   Hmm, that's it. Thanks for reading.